Life Skills for Teenage Girls

A Comprehensive Guide to Navigating Difficult Choices, Conquering Peer Pressure, Managing Money, Self-Care, and More

© Copyright 2024 - All rights reserved.

The content contained within this book may not be reproduced, duplicated, or transmitted without direct written permission from the author or the publisher.

Under no circumstances will any blame or legal responsibility be held against the publisher or author for any damages, reparation, or monetary loss due to the information contained within this book, either directly or indirectly.

Legal Notice:

This book is copyright-protected. It is only for personal use. You cannot amend, distribute, sell, use, quote, or paraphrase any part of the content within this book without the consent of the author or publisher.

Disclaimer Notice:

Please note the information contained within this document is for educational and entertainment purposes only. All effort has been executed to present accurate, up-to-date, reliable, and complete information. No warranties of any kind are declared or implied. Readers acknowledge that the author is not engaging in the rendering of legal, financial, medical, or professional advice. The content within this book has been derived from various sources. Please consult a licensed professional before attempting any techniques outlined in this book.

By reading this document, the reader agrees that under no circumstances is the author responsible for any losses, direct or indirect, that are incurred as a result of the use of the information contained within this document, including, but not limited to, errors, omissions, or inaccuracies.

Table of Contents

INTRODUCTION LETTER TO PARENTS 1
INTRODUCTION LETTER TO TEENAGERS 2
SECTION 1: FINDING YOUR IDENTITY 3
SECTION 2: PERSONAL DEVELOPMENT 12
SECTION 3: EMOTIONS AND MENTAL HEALTH 24
SECTION 4: YOUR BODY AND SELF-CARE 35
SECTION 5: MASTER YOUR SOCIAL ABILITIES 43
SECTION 6: PEER INFLUENCE 51
SECTION 7: MANAGING MONEY SMARTLY 58
SECTION 8: SAFETY COMES FIRST 66
SECTION 9: PRACTICAL SKILLS FOR INDEPENDENCE 75
SECTION 10: THE ONLINE WORLD 83
THANK YOU MESSAGE 90
CHECK OUT ANOTHER BOOK IN THE SERIES 91
REFERENCES 92

Introduction Letter to Parents

Dear parent,

Dealing with teenagers isn't easy. All parents struggle when their young ones reach this critical age. A part of you wants to hold your little girl and protect her from harm, but you also know she needs to navigate the world on her own.

All a parent can do is provide guidance. This book is the best gift you can give your daughter so she can work on her issues by herself and feel independent in doing so.

The book discusses topics covering every aspect of your daughter's life and tips and exercises she will find interesting.

Teenagers are on a journey of self-discovery and constantly wondering who they are. The book empowers your daughter with the mindset and knowledge to discover her identity and embrace her true self.

Teenagers, especially girls, experience intense emotions that are constantly changing – and it can be difficult for a parent to see their child going through a roller coaster of emotions. Your daughter needs to understand the significance of emotional and mental health, and this book will help her learn about emotions – how to express them and how to handle issues like stress and anxiety.

Many teenage girls feel awkward and struggle with speaking up or conversing in class. The book explains necessary concepts your daughter must learn as she navigates the social world, like emotional intelligence and empathy. It also introduces interesting tricks so she can know if she's an introvert or an extrovert.

Your daughter will also learn various skills, like setting goals, self-care, dealing with toxic friendships, creating a budget, managing a household, and having a healthy relationship with social media.

The book is a valuable resource for your daughter that she can always return to when she needs answers. You will notice a change in her when she finishes this book and applies everything she's learned.

Introduction Letter to Teenagers

Hey there,

How's life? You are probably wondering what this book can do for you or how it can change your life. Well, why don't you ask yourself what you *need*? Whatever it is, you will find it in this book. Every question you have about yourself, like "Who am I?" "Why do I feel this way?" "How do I handle shyness or social anxiety?" is answered here. But that's not all – *there's so much more!* You'll be discovering topics you haven't even thought about yet.

This book will take you on a cool adventure. You will never know what to expect, but you will be pleasantly surprised with every chapter.

Like any fun adventure, this book will change you for the better. You will become the person you have always wanted to be as you practice different skills and techniques that can change how you think.

I wrote this book because I understand what you're going through. As a teenager, I struggled with social anxiety and low self-esteem. I avoided eye contact with my teachers so they wouldn't make me participate in class. Sometimes, I didn't understand my feelings or how to express myself.

Being a teenager isn't always comfortable. I want this book to make things easier for you and to be your guide.

So start your adventure now. Let yourself change and become the person you have always wanted to be.

Section 1: Finding Your Identity

Who are you? That's a tricky question. Don't worry. Many people don't know how to answer it, even grown-ups. Some people learn about who they are at a young age, while others discover it later in life. So what's the difference? Well, one worked on finding their identity, and the other didn't spend much time thinking about it.

Luckily, you are here and ready to go on a journey of self-discovery. This section gives tips and techniques to boost your confidence, learn who you truly are, and love your awesome self.

What Is Self-Identity?

Self-identity is how you see and understand your personality, qualities, skills, and abilities.
https://pixabay.com/illustrations/woman-burnout-multitasking-face-1733881/

Self-identity is how you see and understand your personality, qualities, skills, and abilities. Every part of you and your life, like your looks, body, relationships, hobbies, and interests, make up who you are.

So, can anyone define you? No. You are the one who creates your identity using the image and opinions you have about yourself. Hence, self-esteem is key. If you are confident, your self-image is good, and you will identify yourself positively. However, if you have low self-esteem, you will see yourself negatively.

Your identity is made up of many parts. Some people make the mistake of letting their lives revolve around only one thing. For instance, you might only define yourself as a student. Or if you play sports like soccer or swimming, you might identify as a swimmer or soccer player. However, you have a rich personality and life, so don't limit yourself. You are a student, swimmer, friend, daughter, sister, funny, capable, and strong.

Identity is about knowing and defining yourself. So, how can you know yourself? Well, you need to become self-aware. Self-awareness is when you focus on your feelings, thoughts, values, interests, beliefs, and actions to understand better why you do what you do. You learn what drives or pushes you and why you have certain thoughts and feelings.

For example, your best friend is auditioning for a school play and insists you audition with her to encourage each other. You don't care about acting and have no interest in doing a school play – but you agree because you want to support your friend. You both do the auditions, and she gets a role, but you don't. You expected this . . . but still, you're disappointed.

Practicing self-awareness helps you understand *why* you feel this way. Maybe you fell in love with acting while auditioning or wanted to win. Either way, when you pay attention to your thoughts and emotions, you can discover interesting things about yourself.

Be Yourself

Every person is different and unique. Nowadays, social media tries to make everyone look, act, feel, and think the same. It tries to kill individuality and destroy what makes people special.

What is individuality? Your unique qualities or characteristics make you stand out from others, like dressing differently, having a loud laugh, not using social media, or being an introvert. You don't have to do the same things as your friends. Be yourself, and don't hide your personality to fit in with others.

Can you imagine what the world would be like if everyone were the same? Harry Styles, Lady Gaga, Taylor Swift, and many other celebrities made history by embracing their individuality and accepting themselves for who they are. Do you think Harry Styles would be as successful if he didn't embrace his unique style? Would Taylor Swift be one of the biggest stars in the world if she listened to the people mocking her music?

Be yourself and love the person you are becoming. What makes you different is what makes you special. Don't change for anyone. You offer something valuable to the world and the people in your life, so keep being your amazing self.

You can only learn to accept your individuality by boosting your self-confidence.

Self-Esteem vs. Self-Confidence

Self-esteem is how you feel about yourself and whether you appreciate it. If you feel good about yourself, you have high self-esteem. However, if you often think negative thoughts like "I am not pretty enough" or "I am a failure," you have low self-esteem.

Many people confuse self-esteem with self-confidence, but the two are different. Self-confidence is believing in yourself and trusting your abilities and skills. It's knowing that you have whatever it takes to achieve your goals. Self-esteem is consistent. It doesn't change with your mood or experiences, unlike confidence, which can change depending on the situation. For instance, you won't feel confident talking to new people if you are shy or struggle to make conversation. On the other hand, if you are a good student who gets straight A's, you will be confident during exams.

You can only be confident if you have healthy self-esteem. But don't worry if you don't. You can practice certain techniques to boost it and be a confident girl.

Practice Positive Self-Talk

Self-talk is your inner voice or the things you tell yourself. You might think you don't have an inner voice, but everybody does. You just aren't aware of it. You constantly tell yourself things like, "I don't have the skills to do this" or "I don't think I can do this." Whatever your thoughts, you believe them, and they become your reality. For instance, if you keep saying, "I will fail this exam," you won't study because you believe there is no point.

Pay attention to your inner voice and make sure it's always positive and motivational by following these strategies:

Notice Your Thoughts

Everyone has negative thoughts, even if they aren't aware of them. Pay attention to your thoughts and inner voice. When you have a negative thought, change your words when describing yourself. For instance, if you think, "I will fail this test," change it to "I studied hard, and I know I will pass." Or "Nobody loves me" to "I have great friends and a wonderful family who love and support me."

Many negative thoughts start with "I can't," so the next time you have one, replace it with "I can." For instance, change "I can't exercise" to "I can exercise." It is that simple. But it's a powerful strategy that can transform your thoughts.

Talk to yourself the same way you talk to someone you love. What would you say if your best friend told you she looks fat? Would you tell her she looks awful or remind her of everything that makes her beautiful? Use the same attitude and compassion for yourself.

Don't Compare Yourself to Others

No one is perfect. Even if someone is better than you at something, remember you are better than them at other things. So, don't compare yourself to others. When you do, you lessen your accomplishments and lower your self-esteem. Only compare yourself to who you were last year or the year before. Focus on your journey and progress.

Be happy for the people in your life and celebrate their victories. Remember, their success doesn't take away from yours.

The Glass Is Half-Full

Focus on the good things in life. If you only see the bad, it will affect your thoughts and feelings about yourself. For instance, you go to a restaurant with your friends. It's very noisy, but everyone is laughing and having fun. You can focus on the loud noise and have a terrible time, or focus on the good food and being with your friends.

Practice Self-Acceptance

As the name suggests, self-acceptance is accepting every part of yourself, like your personality, hair, body, style, etc. You simply love yourself for who you are and embrace your positive and negative qualities. As a result, you become happier, more confident, and believe you can achieve anything.

Celebrate Yourself

Celebrate yourself each time you accomplish a goal, big or small. Whether you pass a difficult test, save money, help your team win a game, eat healthy for a day, or drink enough water. Be proud of yourself and celebrate it every day.

Write down five things you accomplished last month and celebrate yourself in a fun way.

_____
_____
_____
_____

Forgive Yourself

Everyone makes mistakes; they're a part of life. They give you experience – and you can always learn from them and grow. Don't be hard on yourself whenever you fail or make a mistake. *Learn self-forgiveness and let go.*

Write down something you did that makes you angry on a piece of paper, tear it up, and let it blow away in the wind.

Let Go

You can't change certain things in your life, so don't waste your energy on them. Instead, focus on what you can change. For instance, you can't do anything about your past, so don't think about it and let it go. Learn from it and move on to what you can control.

Write a letter to yourself celebrating what you love about yourself and letting go of what you can't.

Writing a letter to yourself can help you let go of the things you can't control.
https://unsplash.com/photos/purple-flowers-on-paper-DR31squbFoA?utm_content=creditShareLink&utm_medium=referral&utm_source=unsplash

Recognizing Your Strengths and Weaknesses

Every person has strengths and weaknesses. Some people don't notice their strengths, especially if they have low self-esteem. Others feel ashamed of their flaws and often hide them from the world to protect their image. Your strengths and weaknesses make you who you are, so recognize and accept them all.

Make a List

Write down your strengths and weaknesses. Include your good qualities, skills, abilities, and everything you love about yourself. Think back to all the compliments or the nice things your friends and family said to you and add them, too. Take your time with this list.

My Strengths and My Challenges

Strengths are the things I am good at, challenges are the things I need to work on. List and illustrate your strengths and challenges.

MY STRENGTHS	MY CHALLENGES

Ask a Family Member or a Friend

Ask your best friend, siblings, or parents to help you recognize your strengths and weaknesses. They love you and know you better than anyone else. They can open your eyes to a side of your personality you haven't noticed before.

Reflect on Your Weaknesses

Write down three of your weaknesses and take a moment to reflect upon them.

_____

_____

_____

Surround Yourself with Positive People

You are the company you keep. The people you spend the most time with can affect your personality and mood. Surround yourself with friends who lift you up, make you feel good about yourself, treat you with kindness, celebrate your success, and make you smile when you are sad. You don't need people who are jealous of you, constantly complain, or judge you whenever you make a mistake.

It is easy to recognize the difference between negative and positive people. How do you feel after talking to them? If you feel relaxed and happy, they are good friends. However, they aren't good people if they always leave you sad, angry, tired, or make you feel bad about yourself.

Accept Compliments

Confident people accept compliments because they care for themselves, enjoy life, and know who they are. You dismiss your hard work, self-worth, and abilities if you don't accept a compliment. Deep down, *you know* you deserve these nice words because you are a great girl and have been working hard on yourself. So the next time someone says, "You are funny" or "You look pretty," flash a big smile and say, "Thank you."

Don't Be a People Pleaser

Don't change yourself or your opinions or say yes to anything to fit in with your peers. Remember, you are your own person with thoughts, ideas, and opinions, making who you are. Life is about being true to yourself, not pleasing others. If you go against your beliefs to make your friends or family happy, you will be miserable and angry with yourself.

People pleasers help others even if it causes them harm. For instance, you help your friend with her homework and neglect yours. Or you lend a friend your favorite dress when you know she doesn't return the things she borrows. While you should help your friends and be there for them, you must say no when you feel uncomfortable.

Repeat Affirmations

Affirmations are short, positive phrases that are so powerful and can change your thoughts.
- I love me
- I accept my awesomeness
- I deserve good things
- I am strong and confident
- I am kind to myself

Practice Self-Reflection

Self-reflection is spending a few minutes each day alone in a quiet room and thinking deeply about your emotions, thoughts, attitude, needs, and life. It shows you if you are on the right track and if your actions are helping you achieve your dreams. For instance, you want to be healthy. Reflect on your eating habits and lifestyle to see if what you do is getting you closer or farther away from your goal.

Meditation

Meditation can help you self-reflect.
https://www.pexels.com/photo/woman-in-red-shirt-sitting-on-couch-meditating-4151865/

Meditation is one of the most effective techniques to self-reflect.

Instructions:
1. Sit in a comfortable position in a quiet room with no distractions.
2. Close your eyes and take long, slow, deep breaths.
3. Clear your mind and only focus on your breathing.
4. Thoughts will creep in, so pay attention to them and note what they tell you.

5. Notice if these thoughts are positive or negative and how they make you feel.
6. After you finish, write down everything you feel in a notebook.

Embrace Your True Self

You are unique and should be proud of everything that makes you different. Learn to embrace your true self instead of becoming what the world dictates. Let go of people's expectations, be yourself, and do what makes you comfortable.

Be Yourself

It sounds cliché, but it's harder than you think. Living in a society that's always trying to change you into something you aren't, being yourself can be challenging.

You will never be truly happy until you become your most genuine self. So ignore social media, don't spend time with people who don't accept you, and ignore people's opinions of your personality. As long as you don't hurt yourself or anyone, don't let others' thoughts affect how you feel about yourself.

Follow Your Path

Everyone you meet is on a different journey. Follow your path, and don't pay attention to others. Don't try to copy your friend's experience or decisions because you aren't on the same path. Imagine two people going to different places. Will they take the same route? The same applies to life.

Trust Yourself

You don't let your true self shine because you don't trust yourself. You always wonder if you should wear these clothes, speak this way, make this decision, etc. Believe in yourself, even if you make mistakes. Ignore the negative thoughts and follow the tips mentioned. In time, you will learn to trust in yourself.

Get Out of Your Comfort Zone

You won't discover your identity if you always stay in your comfort zone. How will you know what you are capable of if you don't challenge yourself? There are many activities, hobbies, and interests you have never tried before. So, get out of your comfort zone and explore life. Try new things but within reason. Play a musical instrument, paint, sing, sport, dance, or make new friends. Many exciting things are waiting for you to discover. You never know. Maybe you will find a new hobby that will change your life or discover you are a talented singer or artist.

Life is about growing and moving, so don't stand still.

Who are you? It is a hard question to answer, but not impossible. You must know yourself by discovering your strengths and weaknesses and embracing your truest self.

Section 2: Personal Development

Life is about personal development. You keep learning new things, gaining experience, and growing. So, what is personal development exactly? It's a journey of self-discovery and growth where you learn about your abilities, skills, and goals to improve your life.

You must develop certain abilities and learn to set clear and achievable goals to grow and achieve your dreams. Your goals don't only apply to your school or future. You can set ones for personal relationships, hobbies, lifestyle, etc.

Don't worry. This isn't a boring section. There is a lot of interesting information with fun and effective techniques.

Setting Goals

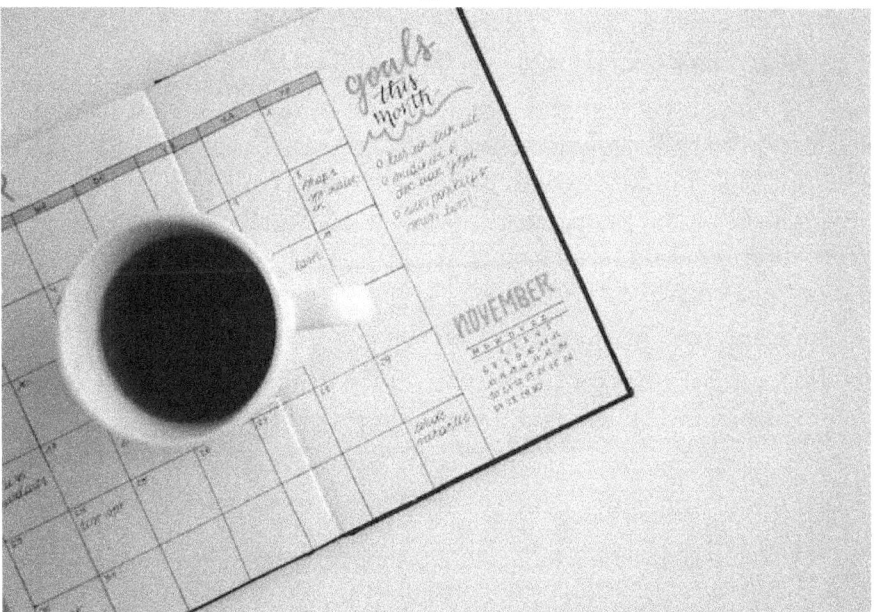

Setting goals can make your life more fulfilling.
https://unsplash.com/photos/white-ceramic-mug-with-coffee-on-top-of-a-planner-aQfhbxailCs?utm_content=creditShareLink&utm_medium=referral&utm_source=unsplash

Life can be more fulfilling when you work on achieving your goals. How can you set goals? It isn't enough to just say, "I want something." You must set realistic goals, plan, and work hard.

Consider these things when setting your next goals.

Set Specific and Clear Goals

If you make large or general goals, you will struggle to achieve them and might fail and give up completely. So, set specific and clear goals. For instance, don't say, "I want to be a better friend," instead, choose to be a good listener. Don't make saving the planet your goal. Instead, focus on recycling plastic and paper.

Set Realistic Goals

Unrealistic goals are impossible to achieve, affecting your confidence, and you will question your abilities. So, set realistic goals with a realistic timeline. For instance, you have started learning guitar and set a goal to master the instrument in a month. This is unrealistic because it is a very short period for a goal that takes years to achieve. Instead, set an appropriate timeline, like a year or two.

Or you want to be a doctor when you grow up, but the sight of blood makes you sick. This is a goal you won't accomplish. Find another dream career fitting your abilities instead of chasing something that will leave you disappointed.

Make a Plan

Now that you have decided on your goal, devise a plan to achieve it, dividing it into several steps. Focus on each step one at a time, and don't worry about what's next. You will feel a sense of accomplishment with every step.

Be Patient

Achieving goals takes time, so be patient. For instance, if your goal is to wake up half an hour early every morning to meditate or exercise, it will take weeks before it becomes a habit. It isn't your fault. Your brain needs time to adjust to the new routine.

Stay Focused on Your Goal

Don't let anything or anyone distract you from your goal. Remain focused. Make it a habit when you wake up every morning to write in your journal or say out loud the steps you plan to take to achieve your goal. For instance, if you aim to ace math exams, you can say, "Today, after school, I will solve a few math problems."

Accept Mistakes

Making mistakes while working on your goals is normal. Everyone messes up, so don't worry about it. Learn from them and try again. You might face difficulties or take longer than expected to see progress. This is also normal. What matters is that you should never give up, no matter how hard things get. Keep going and take every opportunity to learn. Eventually, you will make it.

SMART Goals

Smart goals stand for:

Specific: Set a specific goal to achieve, like exercising every day, eating healthily, or saving money.

Measurable: Decide how you will work on your goal and how you will determine if you have achieved it or not. For example, if your goal is to get good grades, you must determine which subjects you are struggling with or those you might need a tutor to help you with. You should also determine what grade you hope to get and what will make you feel accomplished.

Achievable: Make sure your goals are realistic, and you have the right resources and skills to achieve them. For example, if you can't play an instrument or sing, you can't make a goal to join a friend's band. Maybe you should focus first on taking guitar or singing lessons.

Relevant: Goals that are related to your life and long-term goals. For example, if you want to go to college, you should focus on studying and getting good grades.

Time-bound: Set a deadline for your goals.

Setting a goal isn't always easy, as you may not know where to start. SMART goals can be your guide; they provide an organized plan and simple steps you can easily follow.

Time Management

Time management can make your days feel longer.
https://pixabay.com/vectors/time-alarm-clock-deadline-hand-5961665/

Have you ever felt you don't have time for fun? You are so busy with schoolwork that there is never time to sit and relax. Or the opposite, you have so much on your plate and no time to study.

You always have time. You merely don't know how to manage it. But when you do, your day will feel longer, and you will have time for schoolwork and personal life.

Task Prioritization

Most teenagers struggle with distractions. They are always on their phone checking Instagram or TikTok or texting with their friends. Does this sound familiar? Don't beat yourself up about it. Many people are easily distracted, even adults. Prioritization is useful as it keeps you focused on finishing your tasks and enjoying your free time.

Task prioritization is organizing tasks from the most significant to the least and working on the urgent ones first. You can learn this skill by applying this simple technique.

Fill out the sheet below.
1. **Significant and Urgent Tasks**: Write the most significant tasks you should finish immediately, like homework or studying for an exam.
2. **Significant but Non-Urgent Tasks**: These are necessary for achieving your goals, but you don't need to do them immediately, like working on a project. They can wait.
3. **Non-Significant but Urgent Tasks**: These tasks might not be related to your long-term goals, but you must do them immediately, like responding to a text message or an e-mail.
4. **Non-Significant and Non-Urgent Tasks**: You can do these tasks in your free time, like watching the newest episode of your favorite show or checking Instagram.

Prioritizing Tasks Worksheet

Use this worksheet to prioritize your task or to-do lists. Based on the Eisenhower Decision Matrix, you can easily adapt it to your needs, whether it is for daily or weekly use or longer-range time frames.

Time period _____

	URGENT	NOT URGENT
IMPORTANT	DO immediately ☐ ☐ ☐ ☐ ☐ ☐ ☐ ☐ ☐ ☐	PLAN or SCHEDULE ☐ ☐ ☐ ☐ ☐ ☐ ☐ ☐ ☐ ☐
NOT IMPORTANT	DELEGATE if possible ☐ ☐ ☐ ☐ ☐ ☐ ☐ ☐ ☐ ☐	DUMP ☐ ☐ ☐ ☐ ☐ ☐ ☐ ☐ ☐ ☐

Creating Schedules

Schedules and routines sound boring but are necessary to manage your time. They also teach you discipline to achieve your goals.

Write down your daily schedule in the planner.

1. **Day Routine:** You do these activities every morning, like taking a shower, doing your hair, having breakfast, getting dressed, and going to school. You can make a game out of it and use a timer to see how much time you take with each task and try to finish faster every day.
2. **Afternoon Routine:** Make time for doing your homework, studying, watching TV, and resting. Add how long you want to spend on each task. For instance, spend two hours doing your homework, one hour watching TV, etc.
3. **Night Routine:** These are the things you will do before bedtime. They usually include healthy habits that calm you before you sleep, like taking a warm bath, listening to relaxing music, or reading.

TODAY:

MORNING

AFTERNOON

EVENING

Tips for Overcoming Procrastination

Raise your hand if you have never procrastinated before. Don't be ashamed. Everyone procrastinates. Undeniably, it is a bad habit, but luckily, many techniques can help you overcome it.

Break Down Big Tasks

Some tasks are so big they can overwhelm you, and you keep procrastinating because you don't know where or how to start. However, you can break your big tasks into small ones to make them easier and reduce stress. For instance, if you have a difficult essay to write, divide the process into small steps like researching, writing an outline, and writing each section at a time.

Roadblocks

You start working on a task, but when you hit a roadblock, you stop and procrastinate. For instance, you are working on a project and realize you need a book you don't have. So, you tell yourself, "I will finish the project when I get the book," which doesn't happen until just before the deadline. So, before you begin any task, make a checklist of everything you need and prepare in advance.

The Pomodoro Technique

This technique is effective for working on large tasks briefly while taking breaks.

1. Set your phone's timer for 25 minutes.
2. Start working on your task, and don't let anything distract you.
3. Take a five-minute break.
4. Repeat three times, then take a 30-minute break.
5. Keep repeating the steps until you finish.

Developing Resilience and Perseverance

Life is full of challenges, and sometimes, things don't go your way. However, you can't let every setback break you. You must build resilience and perseverance to learn to get back up every time.

Talk to Someone

This can be difficult for some teens, but talking to your parents can help tremendously. Whatever you have been through, they have also experienced. They have made many mistakes and faced challenges and failures, so they know what you are going through, even if you don't believe it. They also have the knowledge and wisdom to advise you. They truly want you to talk to them. So, why not? You will be surprised by the result.

If talking to your parents makes you uncomfortable, talk to your best friend. They will remind you of how strong you are and give you the strength and courage to try again.

You Are in Control

When people experience failure, they sometimes feel their life is out of control. They might give up and think, "What's the point?" In this situation, it helps you remember you control your life.

Start by taking baby steps to get back on your feet again. Focus on getting out of bed, going to school, and doing homework. Sometimes, doing small things when you feel sad or defeated can become accomplishments. Also, it shows that you can still control your life and have the strength to start over. Once you feel better, return to your original goals and try again.

Change How You Look at Failures

Some people treat failure like the end of the world, "I failed. So, I am not good enough. Why should I try again?" However, failure is a part of life. You failed before, and you will fail again. It doesn't mean to discourage you. You should fail a few times so success can taste sweeter.

You need to change how you look at failure by learning from it. Take time to evaluate what you did wrong and learn from your mistakes. Then try again. Will you fail again? Maybe. However, you will learn each time, and eventually, you will achieve your goals. It is normal to fail more than once, but you must believe you will succeed.

Many actors, like Robert Pattinson and Kirsten Stewart, considered quitting because they kept attending auditions and failing. But they never gave up, and you know how this story ended.

However, it doesn't mean you should expect failure. Believe you will succeed each time, work hard, and hope for the best, but be prepared for failure. The only people who don't achieve their goals are those who give up and admit defeat.

Effective Decision-Making and Critical Thinking

Critical thinking is thinking logically and seeing the situation from different angles to make better decisions. It is a great skill that can benefit you throughout your life.

Weigh Pros and Cons

Whenever you face a difficult decision, make a pros and cons list like the one below. On the pros side, write the advantages of this decision. On the con side, write the disadvantages. After you finish, look at your list. It should be clear if this is the right decision or not.

Take your time to brainstorm. Even ask a friend to help you.

PROS	CONS

Consider the Consequences

Every decision has consequences. Some are big and others small. Before you decide anything, think of the outcome. For instance, you want a dog, but your parents tell you to think about it because it is a big responsibility. Consider the consequences, like the dog peeing on your bed or chewing your shoes. Are these things you can handle? If you can live with the result of your decision, go for it.

Make Thoughtful Life Choices

You should always make choices benefitting you now and in the future. Don't make decisions that will make you happy for a short time, but regret them later.

These tips are effective in making healthy decisions.

- Don't make a decision when you are sad, angry, or feeling any negative emotion. Wait until you calm down so you can think clearly.
- Consider all options before deciding. Take time to brainstorm different solutions and write them down.
- Ask for advice, especially from people who have been through a similar experience.
- Make a decision, but be prepared to face consequences.

Critical Thinking Skills

- Get as much information as possible on the problem or topic by researching and asking questions.
- Don't be influenced by your emotions.
- Set your personal opinions aside and be open-minded. Base your decision on facts instead of what you believe.
- Ask yourself questions or others to get as much relevant information as possible.

Setting Boundaries

You set boundaries to protect yourself from manipulation, people wanting to hurt your feelings, or friends who take advantage of you. They show others how you want to be treated and that you value yourself and know your worth.

Some people might make you feel guilty for having boundaries because they prevent them from taking advantage of you. However, boundaries are necessary for healthy relationships.

Make it clear to people that your boundaries are unquestionable, and you won't tolerate someone crossing them. Similarly, you must respect people's boundaries and not push when they say "No" or feel uncomfortable doing something.

1. Define what boundaries mean to you because they are different for each person. Write down the behaviors you are comfortable with and those you won't tolerate. For instance, you prefer to greet your friends with a handshake instead of a hug.
2. Remember, your boundaries are about you, not others, so only consider your feelings, not theirs.
3. Don't be afraid to speak up and let people know your boundaries. For instance, if a friend wants a hug, step back and shake their hand. Politely explain that you prefer handshakes. If

someone pushes for a hug, be firm or walk away. Don't be embarrassed. You aren't in the wrong, and people should respect your boundaries.

4. "No" is a full sentence. When you say "No," people should respect your decision. You don't need to explain your reasons.
5. Some people will pressure you and make you feel guilty for saying "No," especially when you are still learning to set boundaries. In this case, use phrases like, "No, thank you. This makes me uncomfortable," or "I will think about it and get back to you." This allows you to step back and think about how to handle the situation.
6. Being a good friend doesn't mean sacrificing your happiness or comfort for others. So, if a friend asks you to do something you don't want to do and they get mad when you say no, they are selfish. For instance, your friend asks to help her study, but you are sick and in bed. She gets mad at you and calls you a bad friend. She is selfish, not you.
7. Don't accept people who try to make you feel guilty about your boundaries. You aren't in the wrong. Setting boundaries is healthy, not selfish, even if someone tells you otherwise. Those who care about you will always respect your boundaries.
8. If a friend keeps pushing your boundaries and doesn't respect them, consider cutting them off or spending less time with them.

Treat People with Respect

Treating people with kindness and respect goes a long way. When you are nice to people and meet them with a smile, they will treat you the same way. You could make someone's day just by being lovely.

- Say please and thank you to older people and those who offer a service, like waiters.
- Meet your friends, teacher, classmates, family, the cashier in the supermarket, your bus driver, and waiters with a smile.
- Don't hesitate to help others whenever you can.
- Always put yourself in other people's shoes before giving them your opinion or making judgments.
- Use kind words when talking to people and avoid hurtful ones.
- When your friends or siblings cry, hug them and sit with them.
- Speak in a soft, calm voice. Never raise it.
- Respect your elders and be patient with them.
- Don't interrupt others when they talk.

Being a good person doesn't cost anything. It will make you popular and will draw people to you. Always work on yourself until you become the best version you can be.

Section 3: Emotions and Mental Health

Have you experienced strong emotions recently? Do your feelings suddenly change, or do you have mood swings? You aren't alone. Most teenage girls experience intense emotions. Understandably, they can be annoying, especially when you don't understand why you feel this way. Don't worry. You can get better.

You don't have to feel this way for the rest of your teenage life. Once you understand how emotions work, you can better understand what happens inside your head. In this section, you will discover everything about emotions and how to deal with sadness, anxiety, and depression.

What Are Emotions?

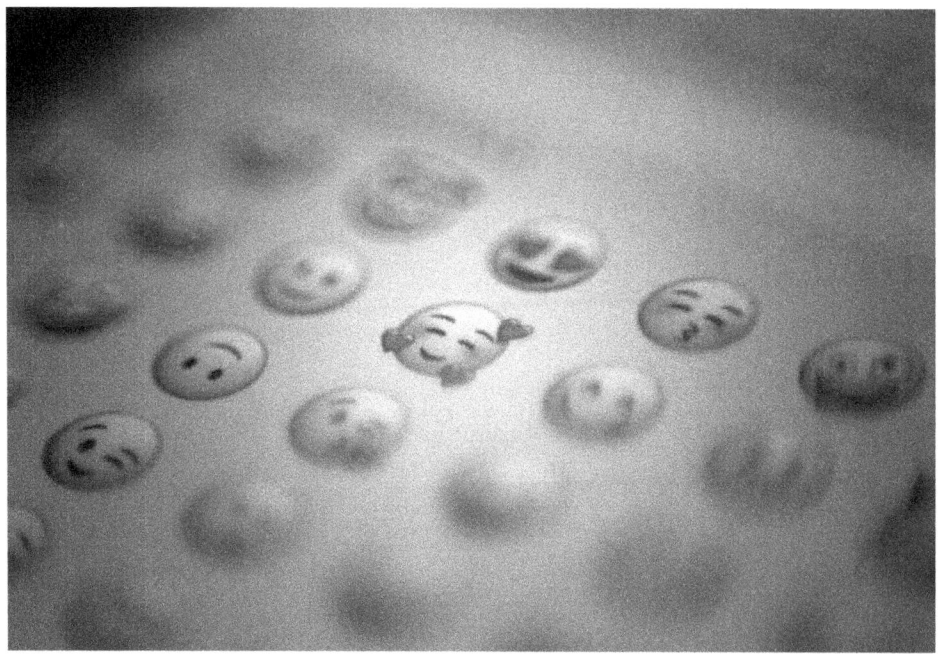

Emotions are how you respond to situations, people, or events.

https://unsplash.com/photos/white-yellow-and-green-round-plastic-toy-Cs3v8Mn6-Gk?utm_content=creditShareLink&utm_medium=referral&utm_source=unsplash

Emotions are how you respond or react to situations, people, or events. For instance, you feel sad when you hear bad news and happy when you pass an exam. You might not know it, but you feel different emotions daily. Some last briefly, while others can stay with you for days or weeks. For instance, if you ace a test, you can be happy all day. However, you can be sad for weeks or months if a family member passes away.

Emotions can be intense or mild, depending on the situation. For instance, you can experience mild sadness if a trip with your friends is canceled, but you will experience intense emotions if you lose your phone.

How Do Emotions Work?

Emotions are your brain's reactions to what your body feels. For instance, if your heart is beating fast, your brain will quickly learn you are afraid, or if you are laughing, it will know you are happy.

You might think your feelings are out of your control. However, you are the master of your emotions, so you have the power to manage them with certain techniques you will learn later in this chapter. First, you will learn about the different emotions you experience at this stage of your life.

Common Emotions Teenagers Experience

Guilt

It's your feeling when you do something against your beliefs or hurt someone's feelings. For instance, guilt is if you say something mean to your sibling and feel bad afterward.

Jealousy

Jealousy is a negative emotion some people feel when they resent others for having something they don't. For instance, your friend could be jealous of the most popular girl in school.

Fear

Fear happens when you feel threatened by a person or situation. For instance, when a dog attacks you, it scares you, so you run away.

Worry

Worry is the result of anxiety and fear. For instance, you worry before an exam because you are afraid you might fail.

Shyness

Shyness happens when your confidence is shaken, or you feel less than your peers. For instance, you can feel shy and struggle to speak up in class if you have low self-esteem.

Anger

You feel angry when someone disrespects or attacks you or things don't go your way. For instance, you get angry if someone yells or makes fun of you.

Happiness

Happiness is when you enjoy life and want to make every day count. When you are happy, you spend time with your friends, care for yourself, and do what you enjoy.

Love

Love is one of the most beautiful emotions in the world. You love your family, friends, pets, etc.

There isn't a good or bad emotion. All emotions are valid and serve a purpose affecting all areas of your life. They are part of who you are, so don't be ashamed of them. Accept and embrace your emotions, even ones challenging like fear or anger.

Emotional Awareness

It is recognizing and understanding your emotions while they happen so you can regulate or manage them. When people aren't aware of their emotions, they express them unhealthily. For instance, you lash out at people because you are angry. You would have realized your behavior wasn't nice and expressed your feelings differently if you understood your emotions.

You can use various techniques to teach yourself emotional awareness.

Recognize Your Emotions

1. Describe how you are feeling without being ashamed of your emotions. Be honest with yourself, and don't hold anything back.

_____

_____

2. Find the causes or triggers behind this emotion. What or who made you feel this way? Sometimes, it isn't the situation affecting you. Rather, it's your interpretation. For instance, your best friend was coming for a sleepover but canceled at the last minute. You will be angry if you interpret the situation as your friend not having time for you. However, you won't be angry if you give her the benefit of the doubt and believe she has an emergency.

3. Pay attention to your physical reaction to the emotion, like sweating, shaking, teeth grinding, uneasiness in the stomach, etc.

_____

_____

4. Ask yourself what you want to do as a result of your emotions. Don't hold back, and be honest with yourself. Maybe you wanted to cry or yell at someone. Understanding these needs makes it easier to control them in the future.

5. Write down what you said or did in the situation.

_____

_____

Label Your Emotions

Once you recognize your emotion, label it by saying its name aloud or to yourself. For instance, say (or think) "I am happy" if you are having fun with your friends. Labeling emotions is necessary to understand what you feel so you can deal with it. It will also make you constantly aware of your emotions.

Express Your Emotions

After understanding your feelings, you should find healthy ways to express yourself.

1. Be honest and vulnerable when expressing yourself to a family member or a friend. Don't hold anything back because they are people who care and want the best for you.
2. Say what's on your mind. You don't need to sound perfect.
3. Express all feelings, positive and negative.
4. If talking about your feelings makes you uncomfortable, try journaling first, then practice talking in front of a mirror and, when you're more comfortable, with a close friend.
5. Before you speak, take a few deep breaths to calm yourself.
6. Accept your emotions and understand there is nothing wrong with them. It will be easier to open up and talk about them when you do.

Developing Emotional Awareness
1. Pay attention to how you feel throughout the day.
2. Rate how you feel from one to ten.
3. Notice how you act when you feel your emotions.
4. Consider your opinions. Sometimes, your opinions are influenced by other people, social media, or grown-ups.
5. Keep a diary beside your bed and, every night, write down the emotions you felt during the day.
6. Discover what triggers or causes your emotions.

Emotional Regulation

It is the ability to know your emotions and thoughts so you can manage them. You have probably seen one of your parents or teachers calm in a chaotic situation. They didn't lose their temper or fall apart. How did they do that? They regulate their emotions. They still get angry and upset but have learned to cope with their feelings and control their reactions.

Sometimes, it feels like your emotions control you. For instance, when you get angry, you can't help yelling. Remember, you are always in control. Certain techniques can teach you to better manage and cope with big emotions.

Strategies for Managing Big Emotions
Deep Breathing

Deep breathing exercises can calm your nerves, slow your heart rate, and clear your head to focus on responding properly.

Instructions:
1. Take a long, deep breath while counting to four.
2. Hold it as you count to four.
3. Breathe out while counting to four.
4. Hold it as you count to four.
5. Repeat until you feel calm.

Grounding Exercise

When you experience intense emotions, you might struggle to be present in your body. You will need to connect with your five senses. This exercise is perfect.

Instructions:
1. Look around the room and name five things you can see.
2. Four things you can touch.
3. Three things you can hear.
4. Two things you can smell.
5. One thing you can taste.

Go for a Walk

Going for a walk can help you release your emotions.
https://unsplash.com/photos/shallow-focus-photography-of-person-walking-on-road-between-grass-ljoCgjs63SM?utm_content=creditShareLink&utm_medium=referral&utm_source=unsplash

Whenever you feel overwhelmed by your emotions, go for a walk in nature. Get out of your head and focus on your surroundings' tastes, feelings, and scents.

Coloring

Coloring is one of the most effective exercises for reducing stress and anxiety. Buy fun coloring books and crayons, turn on soft music, and start coloring. You will feel much better after you finish.

Meditation

Instructions:
1. Sit in a quiet room in a comfortable position.
2. Close your eyes and take a few deep breaths.
3. Focus on the emotion you struggle with.
4. Imagine it turns into a white ball of light and watch it float away.
5. Next, take a deep breath through your nostrils and breathe through your mouth for a few minutes.

6. Imagine something or someone representing love and compassion for you, like your grandmother or a big, warm white blanket.
7. Imagine this warm figure holding and protecting you.
8. Spend a few minutes with this image.
9. You will feel better and calmer than you ever have.

Stress and Anxiety

Stress and anxiety are extremely common among teenagers. You are under pressure at school and home and torn between following society's rules and being yourself.

Stress is caused by external factors like schoolwork or fighting with your best friend. You will experience physical and mental symptoms if stressed. On the other hand, anxiety is extreme worry affecting your life and reducing your productivity.

Stress is short-term and usually goes away by itself. Anxiety lasts longer, doesn't usually have a trigger, and might need a therapist's help.

Stress Symptoms
- Constipation or diarrhea
- Dizziness
- Nausea
- Loneliness
- Feeling overwhelmed
- Unhappiness
- Anger
- Irritability
- Moodiness
- Anxious thoughts
- Fast breathing
- Increase in heartbeat

Anxiety Symptoms
- Restlessness
- Tension
- Nervousness
- Constipation or diarrhea
- Sweating
- Uneasiness
- Fast breathing
- Increase in heartbeat

- Upset stomach
- Chest pain
- Numbness

Living with anxiety and stress isn't easy. However, Certain techniques can help you cope.

Coping Mechanism for Stress

Exercise

Exercise can help reduce stress.
https://unsplash.com/photos/woman-exercising-indoors-hQPTQs7nQQ?utm_content=creditShareLink&utm_medium=referral&utm_source=unsplash

Regular exercise can reduce stress and put you in a good mood. Go for a walk, go running, or play a sport. Choose something you like so you can do it every day.

Get Enough Sleep

Lack of sleep can increase your stress and make you irritable. You need seven to eight hours of sleep every night for your brain to function properly. Prepare a relaxing environment before bed if you have trouble sleeping. Don't use your phone or laptop two hours before sleep. Keep your room cool and dark, and close the windows to eliminate outside noise.

Visualization

Instructions:

1. Sit in a comfortable position in a quiet room.
2. Take a few slow and deep breaths.
3. Imagine your favorite place, like your grandma's home or where you usually go on vacation. It can also be an imaginary place like Hogwarts.
4. Pay attention to everything in this place, like the air brushing through your hair, take in the colors around you, listen to the noise, smell the air, and enjoy the experience.

5. You feel loved and safe.
6. Everything around you is healing and making you feel calm.
7. Breathe in warm emotions and relaxation, and breathe out your tension and stress.

Deep Breathing
Instructions:
1. Sit in a comfortable position and close your eyes.
2. Breathe out and drop your shoulders.
3. Breathe in through your nostrils. Let the air fill your belly and lungs.
4. Feel the air calming your mind and relaxing your body.
5. Breathe out through your nostrils and release your tension and stress.
6. Repeat three times or until you feel relaxed.

Eat Healthy
A healthy diet can boost your energy so you can handle stress. So, eat balanced vegetables, protein, and fruit meals, and reduce your sugar intake.

Anxiety Coping Mechanisms
Yoga
Practicing yoga every day can make you calmer and more relaxed. It gives you mental and physical strength to face stress and anxiety.

Yoga neck stretch pose.
https://www.pexels.com/photo/a-woman-in-activewear-stretching-her-neck-8534778/

Instructions:
1. Sit in the same position as the picture.
2. Breathe in and lift your right arm over your head.
3. Breathe out, put your right palm over your left ear, and tilt your head like in the picture.
4. Repeat the steps four times and switch sides.

4-7-8 Breathing Exercise
Instructions:
1. Slightly open your mouth and make a whooshing sound.
2. Breathe out through your mouth and release all the air from your body.
3. Close your lips and breathe in through your nostrils without making a sound while counting from one to four in your head.
4. Hold your breath for seven seconds.
5. Breathe out through your mouth while making a whooshing sound for eight seconds.

Treat Yourself
One of the best ways to deal with anxiety is to recognize your strengths and accomplishments and reward yourself for being amazing. Whenever you exercise, get a good grade, achieve one of your goals, regulate your emotions, or do anything that makes you proud, treat yourself. Buy yourself a nice gift like accessories, chocolate, dinner, or anything that will make you smile.

Practice Gratitude
Gratitude reminds you of all your blessings. Sometimes, when you experience anxiety, you can't see how amazing your life is or how lucky you are. Put a journal next to your bed and write down three things you are grateful for, or download a gratitude app if it is easier. You can write anything from getting an A on your test, having great friends, eating a nice meal, or appreciating the nice weather.

Depression and Sadness

Depression is a mental health issue that makes you feel sad and tired all the time and lose interest in the activities you used to enjoy. Depression affects every area of life, how you behave, think, and feel.

Depression Symptoms
- Anger
- Ignoring your appearance and hygiene
- Poor school performance
- Social isolation
- Headaches and body aches
- Restlessness
- Eating too little or too much
- Sleeping too much or lack of sleep
- Exhaustion

- Pessimism
- Lack of focus
- Forgetfulness
- Difficulty decision-making
- Need for reassurance
- Self-criticism
- Guilt
- Low self-esteem
- Irritability
- Sadness
- Frustration

Occasional Sadness vs. Clinical Depression

It is easy to confuse sadness with depression, but the two differ. Sadness is a normal emotion that leaves you unhappy and in a bad mood. All people occasionally feel sad from upsetting or disappointing situations. Sadness can be mild and go away quickly or be intense, lasting for days. Unlike depression, which is long-lasting, sadness is temporary. However, intense sadness can lead to depression.

There is nothing wrong or shameful about depression. Many people experience it at some point in their life. Like any disease, you can get better when you get help. Don't hesitate to reach out if you have depression. Speak to your parents, teacher, or school counselor.

Coping Mechanism

If you have depression, it is best to see a therapist. However, you can do a few things to cope with the symptoms.

- If you have overwhelming sadness, talk to someone you trust; they can offer advice and make you see your worth.
- Practice the exercises in this section, like yoga, meditation, or breathing exercises.
- Before you sleep, write down three good things that happened to you, like a friend complimenting you, your teacher praising your performance, or eating a nice lunch.
- Depression makes any problem seem bigger or worse than it is. It is okay to talk to someone when you are sad. However, if you constantly complain about the same issue, discuss a more uplifting topic. It can be something small, like a good movie you have seen recently. Ensure you shift your mindset to something positive.
- Depression blocks your creativity. So, make it a habit to do something creative every day, like singing, writing, dancing, playing an instrument, painting, or coloring.
- Do something that makes you smile every day, like playing with your pet, talking with a friend, or watching a funny video, movie, or TV show.
- Eat healthy and drink plenty of water.

Emotional Wellness Toolbox

Take care of your mental and physical health by promoting a mind-body connection, like expressing gratitude, walking in nature, yoga, meditation, and breathing exercises.

Also, create an emotional wellness toolbox to turn to when facing emotional challenges. An emotional wellness toolbox is a list of enjoyable activities you can do to care for your mental, physical, and emotional health.

You can add many things to your toolbox. Here are a few suggestions:

- Listen to music
- A warm bath
- Do something nice for your friends or family
- Write down a few things you like about yourself
- List your accomplishments
- Look at old pictures and relive warm memories
- Spend time with people that make you smile
- Play a sport
- Do volunteer work
- Go for a walk with a friend
- Ride a bike
- Read a boo
- Spend less time on your phone.

You can add more to your toolbox. Find healthy habits that help you relax.

You can control your responses and reactions if you regulate your emotions. Your emotions are a part of you, so you should embrace and accept them. Never be ashamed of showing weakness or vulnerability. It is okay to be sad or ask for help. It is the only way you will get better. Remember, you aren't alone. Whatever you are going through, your support system loves and cares about you.

Section 4: Your Body and Self-Care

From growth spurts to hormonal changes to shifts in your daily routines, your body is under a lot of pressure during your teens. This chapter addresses these changes, experiences, and concerns during puberty and adolescence, providing plenty of tips, tricks, and advice for navigating this challenging journey. It discusses feminine hygiene and menstrual health. Moreover, you'll learn about self-care practices to keep your body healthy.

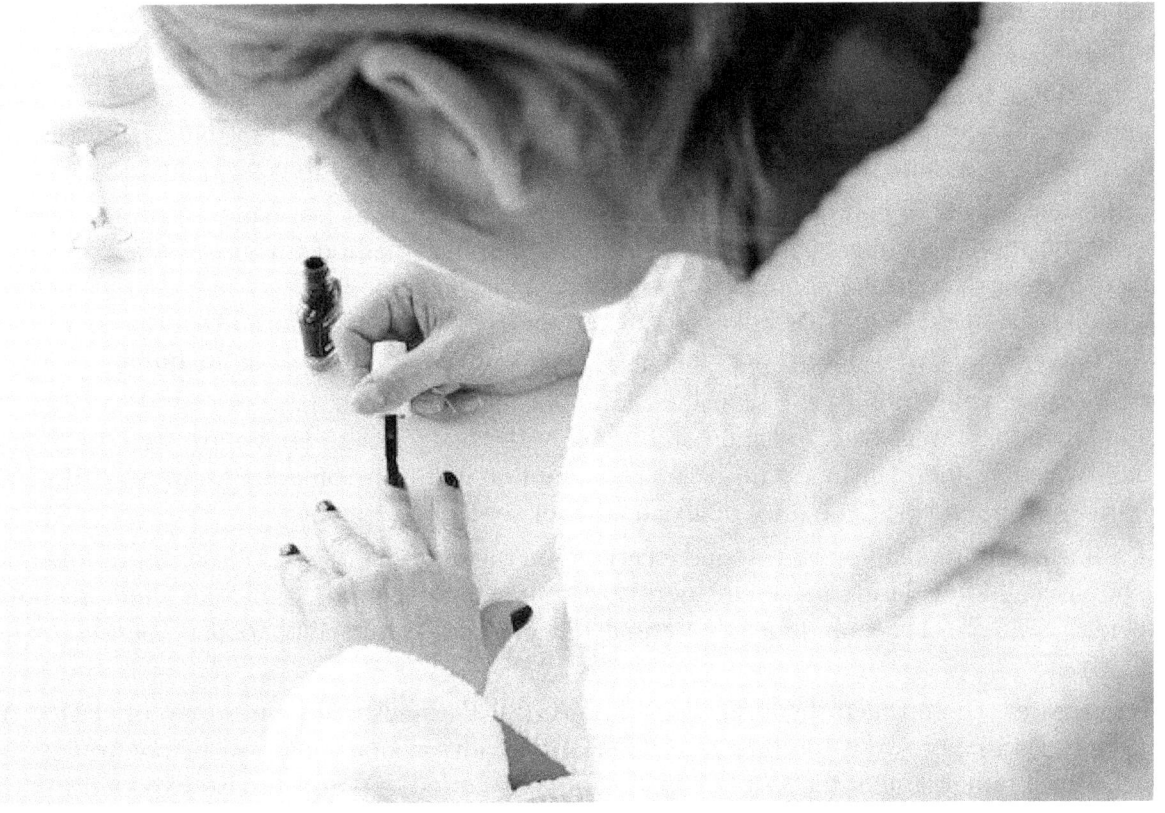

Self-care practices can keep your body healthy.
https://www.pexels.com/photo/woman-painting-her-nails-7321742/

Your Menstrual Health

The biggest shift you'll experience happens when you enter puberty. Most girls get their first period between ages 12 and 15. Some start menstruating at 10, which is entirely normal. However, puberty begins about two years before your first period. You'll notice your breasts growing and becoming tender, your hips widening, and you develop body hair (first pubic hair, then the armpits). Also, you grow more rapidly in height during this period. About six months before your period starts, you might experience a light discharge.

Periods are caused by hormonal changes in your body. As your body's messengers, hormones are crucial in keeping you healthy. The ovaries release Estrogen and progesterone hormones to help prepare the uterus for pregnancy. Each month, one or more eggs mature in the ovaries. Ovulation is when the egg is released and travels through the fallopian tube (a thin structure connecting the ovaries with the uterus). The uterus lining thickens, providing a protective nest for a fertilized egg (fertilization happens when the egg meets a sperm cell). The fertilized egg develops into a baby. When fertilization doesn't occur, the egg and the uterus's thick lining are released, causing bleeding and pain.

While periods typically occur once a month, you probably won't be regular from the get-go. Due to the sudden onset of hormonal changes, you might have irregular periods for up to two years, which is normal. After 2-3 years, you should have your period every 28-35 days. It can last around 3-7 days. Some girls experience short and light periods, while others have longer and heavier ones. Both are normal if they occur regularly.

Periods (and ovulation, in general) signal that your body has become fertile, meaning you can get pregnant. It can happen before you get your first period because ovulation starts earlier. When you become sexually active, practicing safe sex to avoid pregnancy and sexually transmitted diseases (STDs) is crucial. STDs can cause many issues for girls, including long-term health consequences.

Fortunately, plenty of contraception options are available to avoid pregnancy. Talk to your doctor about the hormonal contraception versions, the most popular method for girls. Different hormonal contraceptives work better for some girls than others. You might have to try a few versions before you find the one that works best. That's okay. However, the best way to prevent STDs is to use a condom. Don't feel pressured to avoid using one. It can save you from a lot of trouble in the future.

Just because your friends are sexually active doesn't mean you have to be. It's a wonderful experience, but you must be ready and comfortable with your partner. They must have your consent, meaning you have the right to say no if you're uncomfortable with someone's advances. If someone disregards your boundaries, you must notify an adult or someone you trust.

Bleeding once monthly might sound scary. Don't worry. You won't lose more than a few tablespoons of blood during the entire period. Women have periods until they enter menopause, between ages 45-55. The only time it's normal for girls and women not to have periods is during pregnancy.

Periods are accompanied by symptoms known as Premenstrual Syndrome or **PMS**. You'll experience **PMS** before your bleeding starts. Feeling moody, anxious, and sad before your period is normal. It will only last until the first day or two of your period. You might also experience bloating, constipation, and acne breakout. As your period starts, you'll feel cramping in your lower abdomen.

You should visit your doctor if your periods don't become regular after three years, you haven't gotten your period after your 15th birthday, your cramps are too intense and don't respond to ibuprofen, you have severe PMS, heavy bleeding (bleed through tampons and pads in an hour), or bleeding between periods.

Tampons, Pads, or Menstrual Cups?

While most girls opt for pads for their first periods, feel free to choose whatever method you find more convenient. Using tampons might initially sound intimidating, but it's only a question of practice. If you aren't sure how to use it, ask your mom or an older female relative. Pads come in different shapes and sizes and are easy to use, particularly for beginners. Change the pads every 3-8 hours or whenever they're full. However, they might limit your activities (you can't swim) or make you uncomfortable (they can cause chafing during sports and other vigorous activities). While tampons are more efficient at catching blood (they're inserted into the vagina, as opposed to pads that collect blood as it flows out), they shouldn't be left in for more than seven hours. If you leave them in longer, bacteria can grow on them, causing a life-threatening infection called Toxic Shock Syndrome (TTS).

Below is a short overview of the advantages and disadvantages of pads and tampons to help you choose the better option.

Tampons

Pros:

- Smaller: Tampons are small, which makes them easy to carry in your bag, so you'll never be unprepared when your period comes.
- Discreet: Because they're inserted into the vagina, tampons are invisible under clothes.
- Suitable for physical activities, including swimming: Tampons won't move around during strenuous exercise, nor will they get soaked in water, so they are more convenient to use when engaging in swimming and sports activities.

Cons:

- Might be difficult to use: While tampon manufacturers provide instructions on using their products, inserting the tampons can be challenging, particularly when you start using them.
- Can cause irritation: Tampons are more likely to cause dryness and irritation, especially if left longer than usual/necessary.
- Risk of infections and TTS: Tampons must be changed frequently; otherwise, they can lead to severe infections and Toxic Shock Syndrome.

Pads

Pros:

- Easier to use: Pads are easier to change and are particularly convenient for overnight use because you won't have to worry about changing them frequently. It's also easier to determine when to change a pad - by just looking at it and gauging how full it is.
- Better for heavier periods: If you have heavy periods, you'll have to change your period products more often. Changing pads frequently throughout the day is easier.
- Fewer risk of infections and TTS: Even if they're left unchanged for a longer period, the risk of infection is far lower with pads.

Cons:
- Less discreet: Pads can be visible under tight clothing.
- They can be unsuitable for physical activities: Pads tend to move around. If they shift out of place, your clothes will be stained.
- They can't be used for swimming: Pads aren't waterproof. If you go swimming while wearing them, they'll get soaked with water and become dislodged and uncomfortable.

The menstrual cup is a small silicone cup for collecting menstrual blood. Like tampons, menstrual cups are also inserted into the vagina. The difference is you don't have to change it as often. You only need to empty it every couple of hours.

While periods are healthy parts of your life, you might feel scared (if you haven't gotten it yet) or uncomfortable about handling them. Many girls fear they can't enjoy their favorite activities during their period. However, this isn't true. You can exercise, have fun, and enjoy life as you do when you aren't on your period. Here are a few handy period hacks for you.

Dealing with Cramps

If cramps bother you at the beginning of your period, use a warm heating pad to soothe your pain. Cramps happen because your uterus muscles contract to dispel the lining and the blood. Warming the muscles relaxes them to slow their contraction so they cause less pain. You can get different heating pads in pharmacies or the local grocery store.

You can take ibuprofen for pain relief if your periods are very painful. Additionally, magnesium supplements and a healthy diet might alleviate the symptoms. For example, avoiding food that causes further bloating (like dairy products) will help you feel more comfortable.

Creating Healthy Sleeping Habits

Sleeping less than 8 hours a night negatively affects your health, relationships, and life.
https://www.pexels.com/photo/woman-sleeping-935777/

Do you usually stay up late at night due to having many things to do during the day or because you worry so much you can't fall asleep? Sleeping less than eight hours a night negatively affects your health, relationships, and life. Lack of sleep can cause you to lose focus in school and sports and expose you to illnesses and weight gain.

If you have trouble falling asleep or sleeping through the night, here are a few tricks to help you:

- **Avoid Caffeine:** While some prefer a cup of tea or coffee in the morning, caffeine provides too much stimulation in the later hours. Energy drinks are even worse. They contain sugar, which is guaranteed to keep you awake.
- **Be More Active:** Do you remember how easy it was to fall asleep when you were younger and did tons of running around? While this might become harder as your schedule becomes busier every year, regular physical activity (even an hour of vigorous walking) will help you sleep better.
- **Don't Use Electronics:** Yes, this will probably be the most challenging advice to implement, but put your gadgets down at least 30 minutes before bedtime. Looking at your phone or tablet directly before sleep tricks your brain into thinking it's not time for bed, making you more alert than necessary.
- **Don't Worry about Your Sleep:** Sometimes, when you want something too much, you become so anxious it prevents you from achieving it. It is also true for sleep. Instead of fretting about whether you'll have another sleepless night, tell yourself you will sleep well.
- **Stay Consistent:** The best way to get your body and mind to relax before sleep is to go to bed at the same time every night. Create a sleep routine by doing something relaxing and repeat it every night. You can meditate, read, write in a journal, listen to your favorite music, or spend time with your pet. The choices are vast.

Skin, Nail, and Hair Care Routines

With all the hormonal changes you experience and mounting responsibilities, managing your skin, nail, and hair care routine can become incredibly challenging. However, many teens experience excess sweating, oily skin, and acne. These make having an effective skincare routine even more crucial.

During puberty, hormonal changes cause the skin's glands to produce more oil (sebum). When the excess sweat and sebum get trapped in the little openings of the skin (pores), they get clogged and inflamed, developing acne. An unhealthy diet can worsen your acne. So can your period. Hormones active before and during your period cause the glands to produce more oil and sweat, especially on your face, neck, shoulders, chest, and back. Hormones fluctuate more in teens, so acne is more frequent than in adults, making it harder to manage.

You're likely to be more acne-prone if you have oily skin. Keep your skin clean to prevent breakouts and avoid the accumulation of excess sebum (the oily stuff!)

Hormones awakened by puberty also lead to excess sweating. You might sweat more if stressed. Use natural deodorants and antiperspirants to control your sweating, and shower at least once daily (or after physical exercise). Wear clothes made from breathable, natural materials, as these absorb the excess moisture and let your skin breathe.

Some teens struggle with eczema and atopic dermatitis. These conditions cause the skin to become dry, flaky, and itchy. Their nails might also become more brittle. Sports gear, synthetic materials, and perfumes could aggravate the condition.

Here is how to have healthy-looking skin and nails:

- Always use gentle cleansers, even if you have oily skin. Use lactic or salicylic acid cleansers if your skin is acne-prone, as these help unclog the pores and maintain your skin oil-free.
- Use an oil-free moisturizer daily, preferably with built-in sun protection to shield your skin from UVA and UVB rays. Use a more hydrating, fragrance-free lotion if your skin is sensitive or you have eczema.
- Exfoliate once a week to avoid clogged pores. If you have oily or combination skin, use exfoliants with salicylic acid or homemade ones with sugar and honey. If your skin is sensitive, use an oatmeal-based DIY exfoliant.
- Apply lip balm regularly to keep your lips hydrated.
- Use hand cream to nourish your hands, especially if you have dry skin. It can also help you avoid broken nails and small cuts around your nail bed, which can be painful.
- Avoid touching your face too often. Wash your hands every time you do to avoid spreading breakout-inducing bacteria.
- Apply makeup with clean tools and wash it off before going to bed. Use micellar water to clean your face to avoid clogged pores.

Regarding hair routines, finding what works depends on your hair type. For example, straight hair is easier to style and more likely to get oily quickly. For this hair type, sulfate-free shampoos work best, especially if you can wash your hair every 2-3 days.

Curly hair is prone to frizzy roots and dry ends, not to mention how challenging it is to style. The curls make it harder for the natural oils from your scalp to spread, so you need to use a more hydrating conditioner. Limit your hair washes to once a week to avoid dryness. Use only wide-toothed combs or special detangling brushes on your hair.

Smack in the middle texture-wise. Wavy hair often comes with an oily scalp and dry ends. Your hair might be more challenging to style than straight hair with this hair type. Wash it every 3-4 days, applying shampoo only on the scalp. Use conditioner only on the ends and middle, depending on the length.

Additional care tips for all hair types:

- Trimming your ends every six months will make your hair healthier.
- Avoid using heat on your hair frequently, and experiment with heatless styling methods instead.
- Soak your hair in coconut oil for a couple of hours before washing.
- Keep your hair tangle-free to avoid breakage.
- Stay hydrated and maintain a healthy diet. Your hair, nails, and skin will thank you.

Nutrition and Healthy Eating

You might forget to pay attention to your diet with everything else on your plate. Nutrition is one of the building blocks for maintaining your health and well-being. Girls might develop unhealthy eating habits due to peer pressure or dissatisfaction with their bodies. Regularly skipping meals and eating junk food are equally bad. Food fuels your body and mind so you feel better about yourself. The right food can lift your mood, making it easier to accept the little imperfections everyone has. Everyone's body is uniquely perfect.

You need at least 1800-2200 calories daily to nourish your body – even more, if you play sports regularly. It means you must eat three regular meals and at least two snacks daily. These meals should be balanced, with plenty of proteins, healthy fats, and carbs to help maintain your energy for all your daily activities. However, this doesn't mean you can't enjoy an occasional treat, even if it is fast food or packed sweet or savory snacks.

If you wonder why eating healthy is good for your body, here is what an inadequate diet can cause:

- Irregular periods, often coupled with infertility later in life
- Growth stunt - you won't grow as tall
- Lack of energy for physical and academic performance
- Vitamin deficiency
- Iodine and iron deficiency - more common in girls due to blood loss
- Calcium deficiency, which leads to weak bones
- Inadequate organ development, so you are more likely to develop chronic illnesses in the future

By contrast, if you consume:

- **Proteins like chicken, tofu, lentils, beans, fish, and eggs:** You provide your body with its essential building blocks. Each cell is built of proteins and is needed in many processes.
- **Healthy fats like nuts, sunflower seeds, pumpkin seeds, olive oil, nut butter, avocados, egg yolks, full-fat yogurt, and cheese:** You're getting healthy fatty acids essential for hormonal balance and other metabolic processes.
- **Slow-releasing carbs like whole grains and non-starchy veggies like leafy green broccoli and carrots:** You're fueling your body with energy.
- **Fruit and starchy veggies:** You're getting plenty of vitamins and minerals to keep your body healthy in the long run.

Start with a Filling Breakfast

Start your day with a filling breakfast to wake your body and mind and kickstart your metabolism. It should have plenty of protein and healthy carbs, with a side of fresh fruit juice or milk.

Have Healthy Snacks

Fruits are healthy snacks.
https://www.pexels.com/photo/several-fruits-in-brown-wicker-basket-235294/

Ideally, you should have a snack between breakfast and lunch and another between lunch and dinner. The best choices are seeds, nuts, fruits, and veggie sticks. Everything is easy to prepare and packed with healthy nutrients.

Have a Filling Lunch and a Light Dinner

Experiment and combine different healthy ingredients until you find the right combination. Use plenty of protein and veggies, and align with a few carbs for a filling lunch. Keeping your dinner light is okay, but don't skip it. A veggie soup or pasta salad will give you enough nutrients so you won't go to bed hungry (this, too, can make it hard to fall asleep).

Have Low-Fat Low-Sugar Desserts

It's hard to say no desserts, and you don't have to. There are plenty of healthy alternatives, like fruit salads and low-fat yogurts or desserts enriched with nuts and sugar-free chocolate. It's better to switch to these alternatives than to cut back on dessert altogether because it can lead to craving and binge eating on sugary and high-fat food.

Stay Hydrated

Did you know that not drinking water can make you feel hungry even if you aren't? Drinking sufficient water helps you avoid this and boosts your metabolism to burn more calories. Moreover, if you choose water instead of sugary drinks, you'll reduce liquid calories and have room to eat healthier food.

Liming Junk Foods

Limit junk food (food that doesn't contain valuable nutrients) as much as possible. These only have empty calories, making you gain weight and depleting your body's nutrients.

Section 5: Master Your Social Abilities

Does talking to people come easily to you? Or do you sometimes struggle when approaching new people?

No one is born with social abilities. They learn them from their parents, friends, books, or experiences. These are necessary skills for building strong relationships and handling social situations easily.

Imagine the most social and charming person you know. Do you wish to be like them? Well, you can. Even charm can be learned. You can become whoever you want by learning techniques to make your social life better and easier.

Social Skills

Social skills are how you communicate and interact with others, including verbal communication (conversational skills) and non-verbal communication (body language).

Since the dawn of time, humans have been social creatures. They have always been discovering new ways to communicate. They started with cave paintings, smoke signals, pigeons, and letters. Then, they invented phones, cell phones, social media, and many texting apps. Connecting with others is a significant part of human nature. This is why people always look for ways to improve their social skills to get closer to one another.

Social skills can help you make friends.
https://www.pexels.com/photo/four-person-standing-at-top-of-grassy-mountain-697244/

Social abilities can improve many areas of life. You can use them to make friends, improve relationships with your family, and interact with classmates. These skills will benefit you in the future when applying for jobs. Remember, first impressions matter in professional life, and you must make one people won't easily forget.

The Importance of Social Skills

Even the most introverted people seek human connection. Since you meet people every day, there is no escape from socializing. Social skills ensure you are comfortable in social situations, reduce stress, and are beneficial in future job interviews.

Social skills are significant because they allow you to:

- Communicate your needs easily
- Deal with difficult social situations
- Improve relationships
- Work easily with your classmates on group projects
- Relate to others
- Gain charismatic and likable traits
- Easily communicate your thoughts
- Feel happier with life and more confident
- Get along with others
- Develop relationships with future co-workers

Emotional Intelligence (EQ)

Talking about social skills without mentioning emotional intelligence (EQ) is impossible. EQ is recognizing, understanding, and managing your feelings and identifying other people's emotions. It makes you more sympathetic to others because you know your actions and emotions affect them. People with high EQ can build healthy and strong relationships.

If you enjoy someone in your life's company and they make you feel at ease, they probably have high EQ. These people uplift others and make them feel good about themselves.

So, what makes emotional intelligence so great? Since people with high EQ understand their emotions better than anyone else, they usually control their reactions and responses better. They know their strengths and weaknesses and are constantly working on improving themselves. You won't see them jealous or ruled by anger. In relationships, they always help and inspire others to be and do better.

These people have great social skills and are easy to talk to. They work well with others and can handle arguments and fights calmly.

Empathy

Empathy is another social skill that will get you far in life. You know the saying, "Put yourself in someone's shoes?" This is empathy. It's feeling other people's emotions as if they are yours. It is putting yourself in someone else's position and seeing the situation from their point of view and their experience as yours.

For instance, your best friend is crying because her grandmother passed away. Even though you have never lost a loved one, you can easily put yourself in her shoes and comfort her.

The Fundamentals of Effective Communication

Communication should be direct. There shouldn't be misunderstandings. You must clearly express your thoughts and feelings. It isn't always easy, but you can use certain techniques to communicate your point.

Be Assertive

Assertiveness is standing up for yourself and others while being calm and honest. Assertive people are confident and express themselves without aggression, loud voices, or disrespecting others.

Assertiveness is essential in communication. It shows a strong character since you are willing to stand up for your beliefs and desires to solve the conflict peacefully and fix the situation instead of letting it get worse.

Assertive communication is about how you express yourself. Your words don't hold double meanings, so you are never misunderstood, unlike aggressive or passive people who can never get their message across because how they speak isn't direct or respectful.

An Example of Being Passive:

Your friends want to see a scary movie and ask your opinion. You say, "Whatever you want," even though you hate these movies, and they keep you up at night for days.

An Example of Being Assertive

Using the same example above, if you were assertive, you would say, "I don't like these movies. They make me uncomfortable. Let's look online for another one we can all enjoy."

In the first example, you agreed to do something you don't like instead of standing up for yourself. In the second one, you were assertive, calmly expressed that you don't like these movies, and made a different suggestion.

Clear Expression of Thoughts and Feelings

Your friends and family aren't mind-readers. They won't know what you think or feel unless you tell them. Make it a habit to express your feelings and thoughts clearly without dancing around the subject. Some people struggle with communicating their thoughts. They know the right things to say but don't know how to put them into words. Don't worry. There is always a solution.

Remember, unclear communication can lead to misunderstandings and fights. So, learn to express yourself with these easy tips.

- During a conversation, express yourself immediately. Don't stay silent and wait a day or two to speak up. It leads to confusion and misunderstandings.
- Make your words clear and to the point to avoid being misunderstood.
- Watch people who easily communicate their thoughts and learn from them.
- Don't be afraid of opening up. You will never be able to say what's on your heart if you give in to fear.
- Don't assume the other person will always understand what you say. Make it a habit to ask them if they understand you.

"I" statements

"I" statements are telling someone how their actions make you feel without putting much focus on the action. For instance, you are supposed to hang out with your best friend, but she canceled on you twice the same week. Instead of telling her, "You have canceled on me twice this week." or "Why have you been canceling on me so much lately?" Say, "I feel upset when you keep canceling on me. I was looking forward to seeing you."

Do you see the difference between the first two statements and the last one? The first two sound like you are attacking her. In this situation, she will defend herself, leading to conflict.

In the second statement, you directly told her how you feel without accusations or blame. It allows her to calmly explain herself and apologize so you can solve the problem amicably.

Conflict Resolution

No one likes conflict, and some people do their best to avoid it. However, this is unrealistic. There will be moments when you disagree or fight with your friends and family. It is normal in all relationships.

Learn healthy ways to handle conflicts instead of running from them.

- Try to understand the other person's point of view by putting yourself in their shoes.
- Be calm and respectful. Don't raise your voice or use blame.
- Listen to what they say and ask questions to avoid misunderstandings.
- There shouldn't be winners or losers. Remember, you are both on the same side and want to solve your problem.
- Focus on the problem you have right now. Don't bring up past fights or issues. It makes things worse.
- Try to find a middle-ground, a solution that makes you both happy.
- Once you solve the issue, forgive and forget. Don't hold on to anger or bring it up again.
- Don't keep avoiding conflict. It is better to face it right away so you can talk about it and move on.

Active Listening

During conversations, many people don't listen to each other. They are looking at their phone or waiting for their turn to speak. When communicating with others, you must actively listen. Active listening is more than merely hearing what the other person says. It's understanding their meaning.

Give your full attention when someone is talking to you.
https://www.pexels.com/photo/two-women-sitting-on-ground-near-bonfire-314102/

When someone talks to you, give them your full attention. Sometimes, people will say something but mean something else. You can figure out their intention by actively listening.

Active Listening Techniques

- Maintain eye contact. It doesn't mean you should always look them in the eye. It can make you both uncomfortable. Break eye contact every few seconds and look at other parts of their face for another few seconds, then into their eyes again. It is simpler than it sounds and will become second nature in time. However, never look down. It shows you aren't paying attention.
- Show them you are paying attention by nodding, smiling, or saying "Uh huh," "Yes," or "I understand."
- Don't look at your phone or watch. Focus on the conversation.
- Pay attention to their body language, tone of voice, and facial expression to learn what the person wants to say but can't.
- Don't interrupt. It shows the other person you don't care about what they are saying.
- Understand that sometimes your friend only wants to talk and get something off their chest. They don't want to hear an opinion. They want the comfort of being heard. So, in certain situations, it is best not to say anything and only listen and be there for them.
- When the person pauses, ask questions to ensure you understand them, like, "Did you mean…?"

Non-Verbal Communication and Body Language

People often keep so many things inside during a conversation, but you can read it in their body language. Body language is communication where a person expresses themselves without using words. Hence, it's called non-verbal communication. It includes body language, facial expressions, gestures, and tone of voice. Reading body language is a great skill to better communicate with others and strengthen relationships.

You don't have to be an expert to read body language. Certain signals are universal, like smiling means happiness, frowning shows sadness, eyes wide open show shock or surprise, etc. If you know someone very well, you will always tell when their body language is off – or their tone of voice is different. Just pay attention.

For instance, you are sitting with your friends, discussing your Christmas plans. Each one says what they will do with their family. You notice one friend sitting quietly with a sad expression. You know something isn't right. You take her aside and ask her what's wrong. She tells you her parents are getting a divorce, and her dad is moving out. You give her a big hug and offer your support. You wouldn't have been there for your friend if you didn't pay attention to her body language.

You can also pick up on non-verbal communication on the phone. For instance, you call your best friend, and you can tell her tone of voice is different. You ask her if she is okay and learn she is upset with you but doesn't know how to tell you. So, you talk about it and resolve the situation.

Body language can improve relationships and make connecting with people easier. Merely listen to what they aren't saying.

How to Be More Empathetic

Your mom or dad has probably told you to put yourself in someone else's shoes. But how can you do that? Being empathetic is a great quality that will draw people to you. It shows sensitivity and understanding of others' feelings and needs.

Some people are born empathetic, while others learn it from their parents. Luckily for you, girls are known to be more empathetic than boys. However, there are things you can do to strengthen this skill.

- Understand that not everyone is like you. People feel, think, and behave differently. Be curious about these differences and understand their reasons. Instead of judging someone, ask them questions to understand them, actively listen to them, and support them.
- People share many similarities. Find something in common between you and others and connect with them.
- Socialize with people from different backgrounds to learn about their stories. Do volunteer work, get to know your friends, other friends, and families, and read stories about people from all walks of life.
- When you meet people, think of two or three things you like about them. Also, pay them a compliment.
- When your friend is facing a challenge, imagine yourself in the same situation. Think of how this makes you feel, and use these emotions to support them.

- Empathy goes both ways. Remember to share things about yourself with people to form a genuine connection.

Introvert, Ambivert, or Extrovert

An introvert gets their energy from spending time alone and prefers to hang out with one or two people than in large groups. Think of an introvert like a cellphone battery. They get drained around people and need to recharge with some alone time.

An extrovert is the opposite. They get drained when alone and get their energy from being around people. An ambivert is someone who is both. They enjoy social situations and being alone.

So which one are you? You can find out with this simple test.

1. You are invited to a friend's birthday party, but she gets the flu and cancels it. How do you feel?
    a) Thrilled
    b) Bummed
    c) Devastated
2. Do you enjoy doing group projects at school?
    a) No
    b) I don't mind them
    c) Yes
3. You spend the whole week working on a group project and in soccer training. What do you want to do this weekend?
    a) Stay home and recharge
    b) Hang out with my best friend one day and relax the other
    c) Spend the whole weekend socializing with my friends
4. How do your friends describe you?
    a) A great listener
    b) Chill
    c) A social butterfly
5. How does spending a whole day alone feel?
    a) Perfect
    b) Fine
    c) Nightmare

Results

If you answered (a) to most of these questions, you are an introvert; if (b), you are an ambivert; and if (c), you are an extrovert.

Social Anxiety and Shyness

Social anxiety makes you dread social interactions and events. It can be so severe it makes you constantly stressed, and you might avoid socializing altogether. Worrying before giving a big presentation in front of your class is normal. However, it's social anxiety when these feelings prevent you from living your life. Shyness is feeling tense and awkward around people you don't know.

Certain techniques can reduce the effect of social anxiety and shyness.

- Lead a healthy lifestyle by eating balanced meals, drinking enough water, and sleeping for eight hours.
- Whenever you worry about something, ask yourself, "Are my fears realistic?" "What if something good happens?" "If things go wrong, will this matter in five years?" The answers will show you that your anxiety is only in your head.
- Remember, you don't know the future, so you can't know if the situation's outcome is bad.
- Practice the breathing exercises mentioned in this book.
- Practice the communication tips in this book with the people you are comfortable with, like your siblings and friends, if you are shy. When you gain confidence, make small talk with new friends.
- Practice conversation starters in front of the mirror or with your siblings before meeting new people.
- Before making conversations or a phone call, write down what you plan to say and rehearse in front of the mirror. Expect things not to go as you practiced, but that's okay! You will learn from every situation.

Practice makes perfect. The more you practice social skills, the better you will be. Although it seems there are many instructions, you shouldn't worry. In time, you will get used to these techniques, and they will become second nature.

Section 6: Peer Influence

Throughout ancient history, being part of a group meant being protected and belonging to a society that provided special perks as a member. Safety from predators, environmental changes, and hostile opposing groups were among the many benefits of fitting in with a cluster of individuals. This primal human urge to belong to an assembly of like-minded people has not subsided.

As you grow and navigate the unfamiliar territories of early adulthood, you might notice some changes that further prove the previous concept. You'll find it more common and normal to want to spend more time with your friends than family and engage in social activities with people your age. You'll want to be around someone you can easily relate to and who understands your daily struggles. People your age can easily give you a sense of belonging and reassurance. They can shed some light on troubles you might have thought you were the only one experiencing.

Friends can have a strong impact on your behavior.
https://www.pexels.com/photo/women-hugging-and-smiling-4834112/

The peers in your social circle can have a stronger impact on your behavior than you think. But who are your peers?

The simplest way to explain this word is they are a group of young individuals within the same age group as you. They share similar interests and are a part of the same social class. These cliques or groups can include study groups, sports teams, or colleagues you share extracurricular activities with (cheerleaders, drama clubs, chorus, dance club, etc.). They can also be people who share your ideals and background.

They are people you admire and consider vital to your lifestyle and whose opinions matter to you. These individuals can sometimes act like a mirror, providing feedback and information and helping you find your individuality.

On the other hand, these groups can also be a source of pressure. Pressure is usually associated with negative emotions, but this is not always true. There are several peer pressure types, and identifying them is not difficult.

What Is Peer Pressure?

Peer pressure refers to the action by which individuals within one social group try to influence other members to partake in activities or behaviors they might be resistant to or wouldn't normally do.

About six peer pressure types are universally identified.

Spoken Peer Pressure

The name implies the meaning. Spoken peer pressure is when someone persuades you to do something through suggestions or directly asking. This action usually includes underplaying or overplaying the action's effects. For example, "One cigarette won't hurt. It's not like we're becoming addicts. We're just trying something new," or "Your parents won't notice you've gone out. It's the biggest party of the year. You'll regret it for the rest of your life if you miss it."

If this pressure is made in a one-on-one setting, it might be easier to resist by relying on your observations, experiences, and gut intuition. However, if the pressure originates from a group, resisting the urge to conform becomes trickier, even if the action goes against your beliefs or common sense. For example, "We're all going. We're all taking the same risk. You'll feel left out of the experience."

Unspoken Peer Pressure

This type relies more on the group's actions than verbal instructions. You're not approached directly and asked to break curfew, smoke, or skip class. However, if you are part of a group accustomed to doing a certain action every other Tuesday, you'll likely feel pressured to do the same to fit in.

As a teenager, the sense to control your impulses is usually only 80% developed, so it isn't unusual to go against your nature without carefully weighing the consequences.

Direct Peer Pressure

This form can be spoken or unspoken. It usually involves someone giving you a choice on the spot, forcing your hand to choose a specific path, or being considered rude, uncool, or an outsider. For example, if you're at a party and someone hands you an alcoholic drink or a joint, even if you didn't ask for one, it indicates a requirement of your presence, not a choice. The pressure of not taking the drink and being considered a pariah could cause you to disregard your beliefs and views immediately.

Indirect Peer Pressure

Like unspoken peer pressure, this type is hard to spot. It usually occurs in an environment of people performing a certain act you don't agree with. While you think you're doing the right thing, not engaging in the same action makes you feel left out, even if no one asked you to join. For example, if you're part of a group that bullies others, you might justify the action to yourself that as long as it is done to fit in with the larger group, it's fine. The victims should be better at defending themselves. Similarly, if you're at a party where everyone is drinking, you tell yourself everyone is having a better time than you, and you'll only feel included if you join in the fun.

Positive Peer Pressure

This type is when another individual or group influences you to engage in productive or harmless activities. It can employ the previous methods. However, the difference is in the outcome. It helps in adopting good traits popular within the group and taking actions benefitting the individual. On the outside, it might seem like you're missing out on an immediate pleasure, but in reality, you're learning and gaining skills to improve your mental health, social relations, and overall success.

It can motivate you to work hard and focus. It doesn't involve shaming or belittling for not performing at something or not wanting to.

Negative Peer Pressure

This type is the opposite of positive pressure. Negative peer pressure constantly challenges your ideals and values. It questions your moral code: "Am I doing the right thing, or am I a boring person who's scared of doing anything new." It usually takes you down a roller coaster of emotions and destabilizes your mental capacity. You question things previously established in your lifestyle. It rarely merits a positive emotion, and you're usually left with dread and questioning yourself.

Recognizing Negative Peer Pressure Signs and Being Prepared

Sometimes, you won't notice the effects of peer pressure until it's already started. You'll be swept away initially with the prospects of being popular or belonging to the cool group before you notice subtle changes in your behavior that were too trivial to pay attention to.

Examples of Negative Peer Pressure Include:

- The need to dress a certain way or change your wardrobe
- Justifying cheating or letting others copy your work
- Excluding others from activities because they don't fit in with the group image or aren't cool enough
- Experimenting with drugs and alcohol
- Marketing a different image of yourself on social media
- Being okay with taking unnecessary and dangerous risks
- Trying really hard to fit in
- Comparing yourself to others and compromising your values
- You're irritable. You say and do things you don't mean and wouldn't normally do

How to Plan Ahead of Uncomfortable Situations

If you know certain groups or individuals employ methods to pressure you into doing something you otherwise wouldn't do, try these tips:

- Visualize the situation. Think about how you want to respond. What will you say or do?
- Keep friends with similar values. If you're being pressured into something, having someone around to back you up and steer you away from the influence makes the process easier.
- Examine your emotions. If you're feeling apprehensive about something, it's usually not right. Trust your intuition, even if you stand out from the group.

Strategies to Resist Negative Peer Pressure

Once you identify the situation and no longer want to be in it, you might fear the consequences of backing away and how it will make you look to the social group. However, resisting the pressure becomes more straightforward with a few simple steps you can follow.

Be Assertive

Don't allow others to intimidate you. Say no, and stand your ground. Back your decision with facts so they don't continue to pressure you. You can say:

- No, thank you. I have important things to do.
- I have to babysit my sibling.
- I can't do that. My parents always find out when something's up.
- I can't hang out with you if you keep bringing this up.

You can also deflect the situation with laughter or simply walk away.

Resist the Leader

You have nothing to prove to anyone. In cliques, there is usually an alpha leading the pack. Addressing that person directly and confidently will help ease the pressure from the group. Talk to the leader when they're alone. Leaders usually feed off the group's energy, making it harder for you to drive your point.

Once the rest of the group sees the leader getting off your case, they will follow suit.

Point out that you are uncomfortable and do not appreciate being pressured and pushed around.

Speak Up

There is no shame in seeking help if you cannot stand up for yourself. Asking for assistance from your support system, whether your parents, teachers, or friends, can nurture self-confidence to stand tall. Knowing that someone's got your back limits your loneliness. Their advice can prepare you for future harassment.

Know What Works for You

Trust yourself to recognize what's right. You're not the same as everyone else. Every person has their values and beliefs. That's okay. You don't have to be a part of one specific group. It's easier to associate with a wider range of people with different backgrounds. Branching out can help you discover values you didn't know you'd appreciate and experience positive encounters.

Dealing with Toxic Friendships

Toxic friendships are not limited to a young age. It's more likely to encounter toxic personalities in every age group.

Toxic people usually treat you or others poorly, gossip, are mean, or try to manipulate you to get their way.

People who gossip are usually toxic.
https://www.pexels.com/photo/two-girls-gossiping-with-one-another-6936406/

At the start of these friendships, they strike you as attractive, assertive, charming, and confident people. It is usually the hook and sinker to reel you in.

They say they have certain values and later contradict themselves. They make you work for their friendship, instilling the feeling it's a privilege to be in their presence.

They isolate you from other relationships, keeping you to themselves. Sometimes, there is a hot and cold factor involved. They're warm and friendly – but suddenly, you get the cold shoulder out of nowhere. They use their charisma to criticize you, making you believe you're not enough.

However, it doesn't mean they're evil merely because a relationship turned sour or a friend is toxic. It means they have their struggles and might have hardships you don't know about. However, it doesn't mean you have to stick around and suffer with them just because they are suffering. Wish them wellness and light and move on. Your mental health is as important as theirs.

So, how do you fight off their influence?

- Broaden your circle. Don't allow them to steal you away from others. Be firm and make diverse plans with others. Ensure good people are around you who will stand up with and for you when needed. They can also help you phase out from the toxic relationship without much drama.
- Stay respectful without harming your well-being. Set clear boundaries with consequences for crossing them. Stay kind without losing yourself.
- If you don't want to lose the friendship, find the reasons the relationship is malfunctioning. Speak clearly and directly to your friend about your concerns and the things harmful to you. Do not accept acts of dismissal or threats (if you don't do this, I won't be your friend anymore). Reach compromises that work for you both.
- Fill your time with activities that please you. You don't have to wait for others to do something you like. Figure out your hobbies and put yourself out there. You'll be surprised by the amount of new friends you'll make who share the same interests.
- Get help. If your friend is persistent and not taking no for an answer, ask an adult to intervene or find professional assistance (therapy).
- Remind yourself how being around that person makes you feel. It's not a good friendship if you're constantly stressed and uncomfortable. It helps you stand your ground if they try to manipulate you into staying with them.
- Practice what you want to say to them, "I don't like being undermined and pushed around." "I don't enjoy gossiping. Can we do X instead?" "Can you explain what you mean? I didn't feel good after our conversation."
- Know when it's a lost case. It's not your job to fix others. You can lend a hand as much as you're willing to bear when possible. You need to let go, and they need to seek help if it becomes taxing to your mind and heart.

Nurturing Positive Friendships

What does a positive friendship look like?

Usually, positive friendships are what get you through the hard times. It's the family you choose. These friendships lift you up and bring out the best in you. They're the company you're most comfortable with. The people who raise you up and care about your well-being are honest in their emotions and feedback. Your relationship has no shame, and speaking to them is easy. They share your interests and values. Even when you disagree, there is still room for respect. You don't feel the need to fake your interests or opinions around them. They want you to be the best version of yourself.

So, how do you find and keep these friendships?

- Put yourself out there. The more involved you are with extracurricular activities you enjoy, the more likely you'll bump into like-minded people.
- Don't be afraid to engage in serious, genuine discussions. Friendships are built on the laughs and good times and how you challenge each other mentally.

- Consider the qualities you value in a friendship. It makes it easier to spot those who possess them.
- There is no right or wrong way to start a friendship. As long as you hit it off, share similar values, and are honest with each other, there is potential.
- Be patient and don't give up. Nurturing and finding the right friendship can be hard work, but it pays off in the end.
- Compromise without losing yourself. Ask yourself if you're okay with letting certain things go. Do these actions have a profound emotional impact on you or make you uncomfortable? If the answer is no, then go for it. If yes, talk to your friend about an alternative that works for you both.
- Give and take. As much as you receive, try your best to reciprocate. Lift them up as much as they lift you, and more if possible. Encourage each other to make good decisions and be there for each other.
- Show up for the good and bad times.
- Prioritize each other equally. Nothing kills a friendship like feeling second, or even worse, not being on the priority list at all.
- Try new things together. Go on a trip, take lots of pictures, make memories, or ride a new roller coaster. These experiences mark milestones you'll fondly remember as you build on them.
- Emphasize openness and truth. Don't hold grudges or hide negative feelings from each other. You're not mind readers.
- Respect each other's boundaries. Just because you're friends doesn't mean you get to impose whenever you want.
- Conflict is normal in any relationship as long as you can come back from it without being purposely hurtful.

Remember to seek help when necessary. You don't have to fight alone. Many people and resources are ready to stand up for you. Don't allow peer pressure to trap you in the isolation illusion. Parents, teachers, friends, and professionals are on your side and can help ease your constraints.

Section 7: Managing Money Smartly

Financial literacy is another critical skill you should acquire as you transition into adulthood. By starting early and establishing a solid foundation in money management, you can develop good spending habits and make informed financial choices that benefit you in the future. This section introduces the concepts of earning, saving, and spending money to help you start your financial literacy journey. You'll also learn about the importance of independence and self-sufficiency to achieve your financial goals and stand on your own feet.

Financial literacy is a critical skill to acquire before adulthood.
https://unsplash.com/photos/fan-of-100-us-dollar-banknotes-lCPhGxs7pww?utm_content=creditShareLink&utm_medium=referral&utm_source=unsplash

How to Create and Maintain a Budget

A budget is a plan for spending money. Think of it as money you can spend, and you'll be more likely to set a budget you can maintain in the long run. The fundamental elements of creating and maintaining a budget are tracking income and expenses, setting financial goals, and making informed spending decisions. These steps help you prioritize what you can spend money on and save for the future.

Tracking Your Spending

Note everything you spend in 30 days. You can write it down or use one of the many handy apps designed to track spending. Include all purchases, big and small. After the 30 days, revise your expenses and see how much you spent on specific items. Identify groups and habits you spend on. These will be your budget categories.

Note Your Income

List all income sources, including paychecks, allowances, tips, gifts, etc. Add everything to determine your income so you can set a realistic budget. If the amount varies, calculate an average and base your budget on this amount. Anything above is a bonus that will boost your budget or get you closer to a goal.

Set Financial Goals

Financial goals are anything you want to save money for, like a vacation, college tuition, summer camp expenses, etc. Or, you can aim to put a certain amount into a monthly savings account. Like creating a budget, the key is being realistic about what you can achieve.

Plan Expenses and Make Good Spending Decisions

Create two separate lists, one for fixed expenses (the same every month) and another for variable expenditures (those you don't have every month or vary in amount). The latter is more challenging to predict, so it's a good idea to aim higher than the amount you think it will be.

The easiest way to create a budgeting plan for your expenses is using the 20/30/50 method. Allocate 50% of your income to fixed expenses, 30% to fun, and 20% to unexpected items. The latter can also be put toward larger financial goals or an emergency fund.

Mock Budget

Let's say you have a monthly income of $200 (this could come from salary, allowance, etc.). If you have a savings account, you can save an additional $5 a month, making your total monthly income $205. Estimating your expenses, you need to allocate the $205 toward the following:

Fixed Expenses:
- $30 for phone bills and utilities
- $30 for taxes (after your paycheck if you are working)
- $15 for groceries
- $20 for gasoline (if you're driving)
- $10 to put into the savings account

Variable Expenses:
- $50 for shopping (clothes, hygiene products, etc.)

- $20 for leisure expenses (entertainment - movies, pizza, video games, bowling, etc.)
- $10 for other extracurricular activities (for example, sports or book club fees)

When you add everything up, you get to the sum of $185, which means you'll have an additional $20 left. Review this budget, and then try to apply it to your actual income and expenses. For example, you might have only $150 coming in and no savings account, which removes an added cost. Or, you might have higher expenditures for your extracurricular activities. The goal is to practice setting up a budget so you can start implementing this skill in real life.

Basic Saving and Investing Principles

Saving money is one of the best ways to ensure you'll be prepared for every expected or unexpected expense. By putting as little as 5-10 dollars of your regular income toward your savings, the amount will grow steadily. You won't have to worry about having enough money in an emergency. Moreover, saving enables setting long-term goals, particularly if you put your money in a savings account. It will earn interest, motivating you to spend even more on your savings.

Investing money means putting it toward something that helps you earn more money. The sooner you start investing, the more time you have to grow capital - the money you initially invested. In addition to your capital, the money you earn is called interest. You can invest in stock (a share of a company), funds (a way to invest in more than one stock at a time), bonds (a loan to an insurer who pays it back with interest), and other instruments. You need an adult to cosign with you and help you open a custodial account if you want to invest as a teen. They'll manage your investment until you turn 18.

Prioritizing

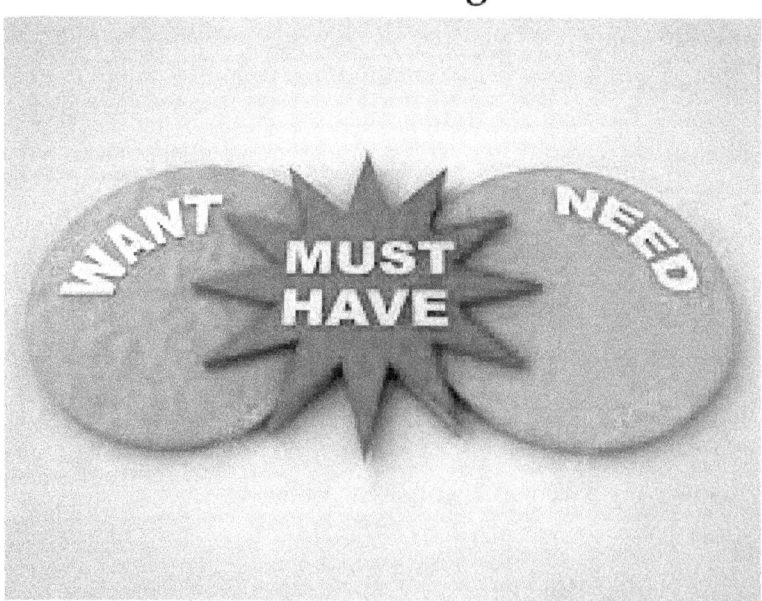

Prioritizing your expenses means knowing how to separate between your wants and needs.
Healthinformatics 1398, This file is licensed under the Creative Commons Attribution-Share Alike 4.0 International license. CC BY-SA 4.0 DEED via Wikimedia Commons <https://creativecommons.org/licenses/by-sa/4.0/deed.en>
https://commons.wikimedia.org/wiki/File:Need_and_wants.jpg

Prioritizing your expenses means knowing how to separate your wants and needs. The latter is something essential you require in day-to-day life, like food, water, a roof over your head, and clothes on your back. The former is something you can survive without. Unlike with wants, you can't compromise on your needs. Prioritizing them is part of conscious financial planning, like budgeting.

To prioritize your needs over your wants, you must set specific goals and create a plan to reach them. Once you have a goal for which needs you want to fulfill and know how to do it, it's time to set the plan in motion.

Your goals can be:

- **Short-Term**: You can reach them within the next 90 days. For example, saving $5 a week to buy a present for a friend's upcoming birthday.
- **Medium-Term**: You can achieve these within a year. For example, saving $10 a week to buy a prom dress.
- **Long-Term**: These take more than a year to accomplish. For instance, saving over $1000 for your college fund.

Banking and Financial Services

As a teen, you can and should open your own bank account. However, you must be accompanied by a parent or guardian and provide valid identification. This identification can be a birth certificate, driver's license or photo ID, passport, taxpayer identification card, or social security card. Some banks or financial institutions might have other requirements, so ensure you and your parent or guardian check what you need to provide the institution. For example, some will ask you and your parents or guardians to provide proof of residence. Additionally, you'll need to pay a minimum deposit to start the account, typically paid by the adults as co-owners.

Depending on the institution, you and the adult co-owner might gain the following after your account becomes active:

- A debit card.
- Purchase alerts so you and the adult can track your spending.
- Setting an ATM withdrawal limit.
- Setting a spending limit (great for sticking to a budget).
- The option to transfer money to a savings or another account.
- A goal-setting feature for long-term financial targets.
- Money transfer capability.
- Goal setting to save for future purchases.

Before opening a new account, ask your parents or guardian to help you find the best fit. The different financial institutions and account types have diverse minimum balance requirements, monthly maintenance fees, and interests. Interest only applies to savings accounts. It is the amount the bank pays you on the money in your account. Savings accounts are for putting money aside, typically for long-term goals. By contrast, a checking account is where you can deposit and withdraw money regularly.

You might be able to overdraft on your account - spend more than your balance. You must avoid this because it means you owe the bank money (the balance and an overdraft fee), another good reason to track your spending habits. You can avoid spending what you don't have. Alternatively, if you have a savings and a checking account, you can link them. This way, if overdrawing occurs, it will be taken out of your savings.

Using Debit Cards and ATMs

ATMs are machines that allow you to withdraw money using a debit card. While all ATMs work with all cards, you'll pay an additional fee if you use one that isn't within your bank's network. Research which ATMs are within your bank's network to avoid this. Most financial institutions have the addresses of ATMS in their network listed on their website.

Having a bank account as a teen has many benefits. It teaches you to budget, save, and develop smart money-making habits from an early age. Being responsible for your account helps you learn to use a debit card, make ATM withdrawals, and use banking apps.

Your Rights and Responsibilities as a Consumer

Knowing your rights and responsibilities as consumers is another facet of financial literacy. It involves concepts like understanding warranties, return policies, and the importance of informed purchasing decisions.

Being a consumer means buying products or services. Your consumer rights are protected by laws governing every purchase you make anywhere in the country. It will come in handy when something is determined faulty after you've purchased it.

When you buy something, you, as the consumer, have the rights to:

- Get products that are safe to use and do not pose harm to you or anyone else around you when you're using them.
- Get products that aren't defective and are of good quality.
- Get products or services that can be used for their intended purpose.
- Get products or services that aren't different from those advertised by the manufacturer or seller.

However, just as you have rights as a consumer, you also have responsibilities. These include:

- Being aware of the product quality before you buy it. If you buy it faulty, you can't complain about it later.
- If you buy items sold "as is," you must accept them with their faults (if any), known as "Buyer Beware."
- You can't demand your money back or exchange the products or services because you regret buying them.
- You can't demand your money back or exchange products if they were damaged after you've purchased them.
- You can't demand your money back or exchange products or services if you accidentally bought them.

These are general rules and regulations. Manufacturers and sellers often have additional buying conditions for different products and services. Some will make exceptions and let you return products or services in exchange for store credits. Or, if you buy products and services and pay a deposit (a small amount you pay to secure the item so it won't be sold to anyone else) and later the full amount, you might get the latter back and lose only the deposit. Always check the seller's return policy, especially if buying something expensive.

Nowadays, there are so many ways to shop. You can buy something from a website, through an app, in person, through catalogs, etc. However, due to this many options, paying for items can be confusing, and, unfortunately, sometimes you won't get what you paid for. So, knowing your rights and responsibilities as a consumer is beneficial and ensures you get what you pay for, and you won't have to settle for items and services you can't use.

Building an Emergency Fund

Emergency funds are money you can access when encountering unexpected expenses in urgent situations. They help you avoid uncomfortable situations like taking money from savings or asking a friend or family member for a loan.

Emergency funds are used for unexpected situations.
https://unsplash.com/photos/girl-wearing-black-sweatshirt-playing-toy-car-flVuw7nbzmM?utm_content=creditShareLink&utm_medium=referral&utm_source=unsplash

Creating an emergency fund starts with determining how much money you want to put aside. Then, you create a plan on how to raise that sum. Here are a few tips for building an emergency fund to cover unexpected expenses or emergencies and achieving financial preparedness for any situation.

Determine How Much You Want to Put Aside

Starting with a small target is best when learning to set up an emergency fund. A good goal would be to raise funds equal to what you spend on fixed and essential items in three months. It can include food, medicine, school-related expenses, phone payments, car payments, etc. Once you get the hang of it, you can increase the amount.

Incorporate Savings into Your Budget

Now that you have a goal, incorporate the emergency fund savings into your budget. See how much you can put toward this goal. It might require you to cut back on nonessential items. Depending on your other expenses, you might start with a smaller amount than you initially hoped for. What matters is that you've begun raising a fund to help you through hairy situations once it's completed.

Automate Your Savings

If you've trouble tracking whether you're putting enough toward your emergency fund, automate your savings by making them go directly to a savings account. Set up an automatic transfer for part of your regular income or ask your parent or guardian (the co-owner of your bank account) to do this for you. This way, the money goes directly into the savings account, and you won't have to worry about accidentally spending it.

Look for Extra Additions to the Emergency Fund

You can identify where to save an additional amount for the emergency fund by tracking your spending. Look at your bank statements or banking app to see where you can cut back on your spending habits. Even if you can reduce your expenses by a few dollars a month, it can go toward the emergency fund. Additionally, consider other times you can add extra money to this fund. For example, instead of spending your birthday money on clothing, put it away for a rainy day. By planning wisely, you'll build your emergency savings up quickly.

Comparison Shopping

Before paying for an item you found in a store, check if you can find it cheaper in another store. The easiest way is using an app showing you the best price from a large database of items. These apps are free. Using them helps you save money and ensures you stick to the items on your shopping list. After all, if you're consciously deciding to check the prices, you're also mindful of spending only what you need. Below are a few more tips on how to do comparison shopping.

Use Visual Aids

If you have trouble comparing two items from different manufacturers in the same store, put them side by side. Does one contain more products, or is it cheaper to buy in a bundle? If yes, and they cost the same or nearly the same, you should buy the one that gives you more products for your money. For example, if you can have three packs of crackers for $4 and five packs for $4.30, you should go for the second option.

Look at Rating or Reviews

If shopping online, check the reviews and ratings of items you plan to buy. It will make you pause, reconsider the purchase, and stop you from impulse buying (which makes it hard to stick to a budget). Look at different products to see which has better ratings. Read all the reviews carefully. Does one product have better ratings and reviews than the other? If yes, buy that one. If neither has a good amount of favorable reviews, skip them.

Make It Interesting

When learning to do comparison shopping, don't start with items you don't want to buy or have very small price differences. Instead, compare items you want to buy. These can be different packs of your favorite desserts. Or a backpack you dreamed of getting for ages. For example, you see a smaller backpack for nearly the same amount as the bigger one. Which one is the better option? Making comparison shopping interesting makes it easier to focus on calculating the difference and making an informed decision.

Section 8: Safety Comes First

This section focuses on personal safety in different contexts and situations. Besides raising awareness about personal safety and explaining how to develop valuable safety-related skills, it also provides tips on creating a safe environment in different communities.

Teenage girls need to understand how to keep themselves safe in any scenario.
https://unsplash.com/photos/woman-looking-at-phone-beside-body-of-water-QofjUnxv9LY

Personal Safety Practices

Be Aware of Your Surroundings

Whether you're going out with friends or walking home from school, you should always have a safety plan. It starts by becoming more aware of your surroundings, like being familiar with the immediate area and paying attention to what happens around you. Knowing your environment is the first step of self-defense because it allows you to notice danger before it reaches you. Avoid walking with your headphones on and using your phone because it distracts you from noticing potentially dangerous situations and people.

Trust Your Instincts

Have you ever heard the phrase "trust your gut?" It means trusting what you first feel in a situation. You are probably doing this if you're in an unfamiliar place and suddenly notice becoming anxious and feeling you're in danger. Your instincts are telling you to seek safety. Learn to trust them by trying them out in different situations.

Share Your Location

Sharing your location can allow people to reach you if there is an emergency.
https://www.pexels.com/photo/person-using-google-maps-application-through-black-android-smartphone-35969/

While using your phone is not recommended in potentially dangerous situations, you can take advantage of its location-sharing feature. If you're in unsafe circumstances, ping your location to one of your contacts (preferably someone who can get you help immediately).

Avoid Potentially Dangerous Situations

The best way to remain safe is to avoid dangerous situations altogether. Here are a few tips:

- Never go out alone at night. Always have friends with you.
- Tell your parents where you are and who you spend time with (it's annoying, but it can save your life).
- Let your parents know if your plans change wherever you go or if you'll arrive home later than expected.
- Don't go anywhere without charging your phone first. You never know when you need to make an emergency call.
- Have a portable battery charger with you.
- Walk in well-lit areas at night and avoid unfrequented places during the day.
- Don't drink or use drugs or get in a car with someone who does.
- Don't get in a car with strangers or someone you are uncomfortable with.
- If your friends engage in a behavior you're uncomfortable with, use your parents as an excuse to leave.
- Get a keychain alarm to alert people in the vicinity that you're in danger.
- Carry a small flashlight with you, or use your phone's flashlight feature.

Home Safety Concerns

One of the most critical milestones in every teenager's life is when their parents let them stay home alone. However, when the time comes, you must ensure your safety. Follow these steps:

1. Lock the doors and keep them locked. Intruders can come at any time of day, even when you're awake. However, don't chain or lock outside doors so your parents can come in.
2. Lock your windows, especially those on the first floor or otherwise accessible.
3. Next, check if all appliances that should be off are off, particularly those you used recently.
4. Keep a fully charged smartphone beside you, or stay near the landline. You should have the local emergency services numbers memorized.
5. Keep a flashlight and batteries nearby.
6. Don't post on social media if you're home alone (especially don't share that you're alone).

Outdoor Activity Safety Tips

For girls to enjoy their time outdoors, they need to take certain precautions for their own safety.
https://unsplash.com/photos/two-women-walking-on-pebbles-9PftZHcnrjQ

Whether it is part of a school program, sports activity, or you're doing it for fun, spending time outdoors has plenty of benefits. Still, avoiding hidden dangers during outdoor activities is a good idea. Here are a few safety tips:

- Avoid approaching parked cars. If you must cross well-frequented areas, always head in the direction of the ongoing traffic. The drivers will see you, and you can ask for help if needed.
- Instead of counting on the drivers to stop, always yield to vehicles. It's always better to be safe, especially in busy intersections.
- Always be aware of who is in front and behind you. This isn't only for your safety, but for theirs too. For example, if you're hiking with a group and suddenly notice the person behind you disappear, you can alert those ahead.
- Always carry identification and a phone with you during your activities.
- If possible, only go on an outdoor adventure during the day. If you're camping at night, wear reflective clothing.
- Only go to well-known locations and those suitable for your activity.
- Dress based on the weather conditions. On hot days, wear a hat and light-colored clothes. On cold days, layer up in sweat-wicking clothes and wear gloves and winter hats.

- Wear shoes suitable for the activity. Make sure they fit well and have good support in the right places.
- Only embark on activities you feel physically fit for and adjust your moving speed to your abilities.
- Stretch and warm up before vigorous activities.
- Avoid outdoor activities if you're injured or experience severe pain. Besides aggravating your condition, it could also make you vulnerable to attackers.

General Physical Safety Tips

Besides those listed above, here are a few additional physical safety tips:

- Don't get close to, speak, or interact with strangers, especially if they seem suspicious.
- Avoid hitchhiking. Only get in the car with people you know. Even then, check if the doors remain locked.
- If you're with someone whose behavior makes you uncomfortable, have your phone ready to call for help. Bring up an emergency service number or one of your emergency contacts.
- If you feel unsafe at any location, call your parents or another adult you trust and loudly describe where you are, who is around you, and your current situation.
- If you feel unsafe and are alone, pretend there is someone else in the area by calling out to them to fool potential attackers into thinking you aren't alone.
- If someone tries to grab you and pull you inside a building or vehicle, do your best to fight them off or run.
- Don't accept gifts from strangers, and don't believe their excuses to get you inside their home or vehicle. For example, they might offer money or invite you to see their pet.

Self-defense techniques should be a priority for all teenage girls.
Image by svklimkin from Pixabay https://pixabay.com/photos/karate-sunset-fight-sports-2578819/

Self-Defense Techniques

Learning basic self-defense techniques is another great way to fend off potential attackers. As you'll see below, self-defense isn't only about defending yourself physically.

Start with the Right Mannerism and Body Language

Walking with your head up has several benefits. It helps you be more aware and look more confident. Don't slouch or drag your feet. Walk straight and keep your hands beside you instead of your pockets so you won't look like an easy target.

Control the Distance

Controlling the distance between you and your attacker is the best way to remain unharmed:

1. Try keeping a steady distance between yourself and the attacker whenever possible.
2. Have at least one object between you, stay outside of reaching distance, and hold your arms in front of you if you need to defend yourself.
3. Keep moving, but only start defending yourself when necessary.
4. Stop trying to move away if your attacker is close enough to strike you. Instead, get as close to their body as possible. It will make it harder for them to hit you.
5. As they try to maneuver around you, look for signs of them losing their balance. For example, if they stand on one leg or lean in one direction. Try tripping them as soon as you notice.
6. Once you've tripped them and they fall to the ground, run.

Assuming a Fight Stance

Assuming a good fight stance is your next best option if you can't trip or get away from the attacker.

To have a good fight stance, you must find your balance and have a plan to protect yourself:

1. Keep your head up to keep your eyes on the attacker.
2. Stand with your feet shoulder-width apart, one foot behind the other, facing the attacker.
3. The front part of your hips must face your attacker.
4. Bend your knees slightly and shift your weight to the balls of your feet so you can move quickly.
5. Bring your hands up in front to protect your face.
6. Keep your elbows by your sides to shield your ribs and internal organs.
7. Move around to make it harder for the attacker to strike you.

Breaking Grips

Grabbing and using a tight grip to control them is a common way attackers overpower girls. Fortunately, there are ways to break free from grips. The key is to expose and track the weakest part of their grip.

Instructions:

1. Move around to make it harder for the attacker to maintain their grip on you.
2. Once their grip is weakened, use two hands to try to break it.
3. Try to remove or strike their fingers, as these are the weakest points.
4. Continue pushing and pulling with your entire body to loosen their grip until you can break free.

Recognizing Signs of Unhealthy or Abusive Relationships

Recognizing you're in a toxic relationship can be even more challenging for teens than adults. Here are the signs to look for:

- **Physical and Verbal Abuse**: If the other person puts you down, calls you names, threatens to harm you or themselves, or even hurts you physically, it is a sure sign of an unhealthy relationship.
- **Quick Commitment**: If you or the person is too quick to say you'll never leave or can't live without each other, these are also warning signs.
- **Extreme Highs and Lows**: Something is wrong if you're extremely happy or unhappy during the relationship.
- **Isolation**: If you notice you stopped hanging out with your friends and family and neglecting your hobbies to please the other person (whether they asked you or not), you're likely in an unhealthy relationship.

Setting Boundaries in Relationships

If you feel uncomfortable or unsafe being around someone, put some distance between you. It might seem rude, but it's always better to do it and protect yourself than hesitate and get hurt. No matter how long you know someone and your relationship with them, there should always be boundaries between you. Explain clearly what you're comfortable with and what behavior you won't tolerate. If they disrespect your boundaries, distance yourself from them as much as possible.

Emergency Preparedness

Being prepared for emergencies is another way to remain safe. For example, you should know to call emergency services when:

- Someone becomes unconscious after drinking too much or getting into an accident.
- Someone feels dizzy, nauseous, and disoriented after an accident or eating or drinking something.
- Someone starts choking, has a seizure, or has trouble breathing due to a condition like asthma or allergies.
- You notice a fire or a crime, like someone getting mugged.
- You're in or see an accident of any sort.

If and when you call emergency services, be prepared to explain what happened, where you are or where you live, who is with you, and who needs help. Remain calm and speak slowly so the operators can understand you.

If someone's been hurt, don't move them or try to clean their wounds. If they're bleeding, put pressure on their injuries if possible. If they're in an unsafe place, don't approach them to avoid putting yourself in danger.

If you're around someone who takes medication (or you take medication), always keep these (along with insurance information) at hand.

Here are a few tips on what to do in case of natural disasters:
- **Severe Thunderstorms:** Stay indoors and avoid using or staying near electrical outlets or running water as they conduct electricity.
- **Tornados:** When inside, go to the building's lowest level and stay away from doors, windows, and walls. If outside, stay clear of buildings, find a low area to lie down, and protect your head with your hands.
- **Earthquakes:** Identify the safest places in every room (away from anything that might fall, as with tornadoes). When the tremors start, drop, cover your head, and hold onto something.
- **Hurricanes:** Stay away from glass doors and windows and find cover in the lowest area of the home.
- **Floods:** Avoid areas of at least six inches of water. The water flow can knock you over, and you won't see the sharp objects the water might carry, not to mention the bacteria and other microbes that could make you very ill.

Building a Safety Plan

To avoid being unprepared, have a safety plan for emergencies.

Some general advice includes:
- **Figuring Out How to Stay Connected with Your Family:** In a major emergency, mobile phones will not work, so you must find another way to stay in touch if you aren't with them. For example, you can have a designated area where everyone can meet safely after disaster strikes.
- **Learning Basic Emergency Skills:** If you don't have adults around during a disaster, you can only rely on yourself to remain safe or save yourself from harm. Learning to use a fire extinguisher, applying first aid, or knowing how to get around without transportation are a few of the most recommended emergency skills.

Do you know what else is useful to help execute your emergency plan? An emergency kit. Here is how to put together a kit for any emergencies, big or small:

1. Find a bag big enough to fit all the supplies. The more compartments, the better. However, the bag shouldn't be too heavy.
2. Get some smaller cases, too, like makeup bags with zippers to organize what you put in the larger bag. Label them so you can find everything during an emergency.
3. First, put emergency money in the bag. Change is the best because you can use it for a payphone (in case mobile phones don't work). Place it in a pocket with a zipper for safety.
4. If you take medication, these go next. Pack an Epi-Pen in the bag if you have severe allergies. Eye drops and a first aid kit will also come in handy. Keep the meds in a separate pocket.
5. If you're making your first aid kit, include adhesives, tweezers, antiseptic wipes and hand sanitizers, tissues, pain relief medication, cough drops, and throat lozenges.
6. Don't forget your period products. Pack plenty of your preferred products and an extra pair of underwear.
7. Pack water and some snacks (nonperishable, prepackaged food items). Think nuts, granola bars, crackers, etc.

8. If you wear contacts or glasses, putting an extra pair into your emergency kit is a good idea in case you lose the others. Don't forget to include a cleaning solution for the contacts.
9. In a re-sealable bag, prepare a change of clothes, including pants, a T-shirt, bra, and socks.
10. Next are the travel toiletries. While small in size, these can be a lifesaver in emergencies. Not only will they help you freshen up, but staying clean is also an excellent way to prevent infections and other diseases.
11. A small sewing kit might also be handy if you need to repair your clothes or someone else's.
12. Ensure that you put paper, a pen, and a few paper clips inside the bag. You might need to write something down.
13. Lastly, it's a good idea to pack a second phone charger in the bag in case you lose the other one while moving during an emergency or disaster.

Creating Safe Spaces

Besides staying safe on your own, you can also create safe spaces for others within your school, online, or in other communities. Even if it's only a girls' club, it can still serve to support one another because every girl has the right to feel safe anywhere and anywhere. Talk to your friends about everyone's concerns regarding expressing themselves and devise a plan to resolve these issues. Whether these problems concern online safety or a school environment, focus your efforts on where you can help the most.

A girls' group can help everyone feel safe, not to mention a great way to socialize. You can share your experiences and help each other with resources regarding female health and other topics. The idea is to create a space where everyone can talk about anything without judgment. You can create a group doing a joint activity everyone enjoys. Nothing helps express yourself more than engaging with friends with similar problems in a fun activity.

A safe space for girls builds their social skills. Even if some aren't too confident in social situations, knowing you'll be understood will encourage you to come out of your shell. Whether someone struggles with a mental health disorder, eating disorder, or other condition, creating a safe space to share their concerns can help them overcome their issues. You gain a broader range of social skills as you talk among yourself on whichever platform or channel you choose to communicate. These are only a few suggestions for creating a safe space for girls. Feel free to advocate for your topics.

Section 9: Practical Skills for Independence

This section outlines comprehensive practical life skills to thrive as a self-reliant and confident individual. You'll learn the importance of mastering cooking and house management, first aid, job, and navigation. They're necessary for a seamless transition into independent adulthood.

Cooking Skills and Nutrition Basics

Cooking is a fundamental skill for an independent and self-sufficient life. By learning how to cook your meals, you can save money and eat healthier. You'll learn nutrition basics and what ingredients to use to create balanced meals.

Grocery Shopping

A grocery list can help you recognize what you need to buy.
https://unsplash.com/photos/a-notepad-with-a-green-pen-sitting-on-top-of-it-CIFbCe4L_pw?utm_content=creditShareLink&utm_medium=referral&utm_source=unsplash

Every cooking journey starts with grocery shopping. Always make a list of items to buy for several meals or days. This way, you won't have to make too many trips or buy too much or too little produce at a time.

Basic Knife and Measuring Skills

Ask an adult to explain the purpose of the different knives and how to use them properly. Larger ones can be scary to handle, but you can make cooking much easier with practice.

Familiarize yourself with the different measuring cups and spoons and practice measuring dry and liquid ingredients.

Using Kitchen Appliances

Knowing how to use a slow cooker, a microwave, or an instant pot can be handy when working or studying and don't have much time to spend in the kitchen.

Reading, Following, and Modifying Recipes

Ask yourself questions when reading recipes. What ingredients do you need? How much of each? In what order to use them? If necessary, read the recipe several times until you have answers to your questions. Once you get the hang of following directions, you can start experimenting with cutting and doubling recipes. Doubling will help you make big batches to freeze for later. Unlike ready-made versions, frozen home-cooked meals only contain good ingredients without unhealthy additives like preservatives, food coloring, and taste enhancers.

Prepping

Preparing everything to cook a meal will make the process easier. Read the recipe to see what you need, gather everything, and only then start cooking. This way, you won't have to stop countless times to hunt down the ingredients or tools.

Making Healthy Snacks

The easiest way to make healthy snacks is to combine nuts and dried fruit and create your own trail mix. You can also make granola by combining dried rolled oats with nuts, chopped dates, and enough liquids so everything sticks together. Lay it on a flat surface and put it in the fridge overnight, and you'll have a nutritious snack.

Making Salad and Soups

Salads are one of the healthiest meals and are easy to put together. You can experiment with different ingredients, including veggies, fruits, protein, and carbs. Have you ever tried making homemade croutons? Cut bread into pieces, season it with oil and herbs, and toast it in the oven until your croutons are ready.

Soups are equally simple to make and quite filling. Start with a cream-or-broth-based soup recipe, where you only need to add the other ingredients to a base and cook until done.

Making One-Pot Meals and Casseroles

One-pot meals and casseroles are the easiest ways to create nutritious, filling meals. You only need to learn a few basic recipes for these dishes to know which ingredients to layer in the tray or dump into the pot.

Cooking Meat and Eggs

Find recipes for ground beef. It's a great way to practice cooking meat. You can make meatloaf, hamburgers, or anything you like.

You should also learn to pan-fry, roast and grill, and cook breakfast meats. Learning to scramble, boil, fry, and poach eggs or make an omelet gives you even more breakfast options and saves money on getting breakfast at a fast food place.

Cooking Veggies

Vegetables are full of healthy macronutrients and can be prepared in many ways. Roasting veggies is the simplest method, but boiling them is equally convenient. Practice how to determine when your veggies are fork-tender.

Time-Management and Storing

Knowing when to start preparing and making the different elements of a recipe is fundamental for success in the kitchen. Practice when to add the ingredients to the meal to cook them appropriately and manage your time efficiently.

If you cook bigger batches, portion the leftovers and freeze them. Consider the portion sizes based on how much you normally eat (if you're cooking for someone else, consider their portions) and measure them in separate containers.

Household Management

With everything else on your plate, cleaning and maintaining a household might be the last thing you'll think of. However, organizing your space helps you become more productive and waste less time and money. It's an essential skill for establishing your independence in the future. Below are some tips on creating and maintaining a clean and functional living space:

Make Cleaning, Tidying, and Decluttering a Regular Habit

Regular cleaning, tidying, and decluttering sessions help you prevent clutter and grime from accumulating and make you think of these activities as less of a chore. Wouldn't you rather spend 10-15 minutes daily doing them than deal with the mess for hours after everything has piled up for weeks? Set reminders on your phone for cleaning at a convenient time. For example, if you are a morning person, you might find it the easiest to do it after waking up. Night owls will surely prefer tidying up in the evening. Set a timer so you know when to stop. After a while, it'll become a habit, and you won't need reminders or timers anymore.

If you have trouble getting started, here is a daily and weekly schedule to inspire you:

Daily Tasks:

- Putting dirty clothes into the laundry basket
- Cleaning dirty plates and glasses
- Putting clean laundry away
- Making beds and tidying up spaces
- Ensuring the floor is clean
- Putting away your makeup and craft material
- Organizing your school bag and materials

Weekly Tasks:

- Tiding desks

- Dusting and vacuuming
- Changing bedding
- Emptying laundry baskets
- Doing the laundry

Make It fun

It's hard to get into the habit of regular cleaning, decluttering, and tidying if you view these as boring tasks you must complete. Playing some music can make it a fun experience, but be careful not to get distracted. You'll be amazed at the results.

Find Efficient Storage Solutions

Efficient storage solutions will make cleaning up and maintaining order easier and faster. You can start practicing by organizing your room. Pick the solution that works for you. For example, if you prefer to throw things into their places quickly, you'll need bigger containers. Whereas, if you like to sort your belongings into different categories, use small containers and other storage solutions with dividers. Label everything clearly, and place them into easily accessible areas. Later on, you can also implement the same tactics to organize the bathroom and other areas of the home.

Handling Laundry

Laundry baskets are essential in every room. Instead of tripping on dirty clothes lying around the floor or sorting through clothing hanging over chairs, they can be safely "hidden" in a laundry basket tucked in the corner of the room. Throwing clothes into them is just as easy as throwing them on the floor, but the space will look much tidier. In addition to the individual rooms' baskets, every household should have a main basket in the laundry room. Make it a habit of regularly emptying the smaller ones into the main ones. When the latter gets full, wash the clothes. Don't forget to sort them before washing as not all clothes can be washed at the same temperature.

Garbage Bins

The same laundry basket rules apply to garbage bins. Have a small one in every room, and empty it regularly. Taking out the garbage helps prevent pest issues (bugs and critters are usually attracted by the smell).

Maximize Storage

Using hidden storage areas and vertical space are excellent ways to create more storage in every room. For example, you can have drawers (even plastic ones, especially for those on a tight budget) under beds, sinks, tables, etc. Vertical storage spaces are practical for doors, wardrobes, kitchen walls, and similar areas. You would be surprised how much extra space you can create by sticking a few pegs and hooks onto a door or wall. You can hang up many items so they won't lie on the floor.

Keep All Surfaces Clean

Keeping floors clean is a no-brainer. If someone falls due to a spill or mess you failed to clean, they can seriously hurt themselves. Also, keep the clutter to a minimum on other surfaces (start with the shelves in your room, then implement this in other areas) to make cleaning and tidying up easier.

Basic First-Aid Skills

Basic first-aid skills are always useful because you never know when you or someone else could get hurt. Below are some of the most fundamental skills:

Stopping a Bleed

If you or someone else gets hurt and starts bleeding, here is what you can do to stop it:

1. Take a cloth or bandage, bundle it in your hand, and press it on the scrape or cut. If you can't find any material, use only your hands to apply pressure.
2. Hold the makeshift bandage on the wound for several minutes. Check after five minutes if the bleeding has stopped.
3. If blood seeps through the cloth or bandage, place another layer on top.
4. Call emergency services if the bleeding doesn't stop or the wound is too deep.

Treating Small Burns

If you or someone else burns themselves handling a hot appliance, like an iron, hot hair tool, or oven, here is what you can do to cool a burn:

1. Go to the nearest tap or running water source and place the burned area under the water line. Keep the water cold.
2. If the skin's edges in the burned area are peeling, you can remove them.
3. Put a thick layer of aloe vera gel or a similarly cooling lotion or cream onto the burn.
4. Wet a towel or clean cloth and place it on the burn. Tell an adult or call emergency services if the burned area is very big and painful.

Treating a Nosebleed

Nosebleeds are relatively easy to stop if you follow these steps:

1. Sit and lean slightly forward.
2. Using your thumb and index finger, pinch both sides of your nose at the nostrils. Press your fingers tightly. It helps stop the blood flow and the bleeding.
3. Check if the bleeding has stopped after several minutes. If the nose is still bleeding after 15 minutes, call emergency services.

CPR

If someone has a heart attack or their heart stops for any reason, CPR can help it restart.

Here is how to perform CPR:

1. Before you start CPR, check if the person has a pulse and if they're breathing. Check for a pulse by pressing two fingers on the side of the person's neck. Check if their chest rises and falls to see if they're breathing. Alternatively, you can place a piece of glass, a mirror, or even your phone under their nose - if the glass surface gets clouded, the person is breathing.
2. If you can't find a pulse and the person isn't breathing, it's time to start CPR.
3. Press down on their chest 30 times. This movement is known as chest compression.
4. Pinch their nose to stop the air from escaping and blow two breaths into their mouth.
5. Repeat steps #3 and #4 until help arrives.

How to Read Medication Labels

Most over-the-counter medication has a label indicating what the medicine is for and how to use it.

Here are the different elements on a medication label:

- **Active Ingredients:** This section enlists ingredients making up the medication.
- **Purpose:** This section tells you what the active component does.
- **Uses:** This shows the symptoms the medicine can treat. This and the previous section combined determine whether you can take or give the medication to someone based on the symptoms.
- **Warnings:** This part enlists other medicines and conditions, making this medication ill-advised.
- **Directions:** This section indicates how to take the medicine, including how often, how long, and how much a person can take.
- **Other Information:** This part tells you how to store the medication and has additional information about the ingredients.
- **Inactive Ingredients:** This is a list of inactive ingredients in the body. However, they can cause an allergic reaction, so they shouldn't be given to a person allergic to them.

How to Choose Your First Job

Choosing your first job can be challenging. Here are some tips to help you make the best choice:

- **Set Goals:** Establish realistic goals about how much work you can do while juggling other obligations. Some jobs require minimum working hours per week. Also, consider travel time.
- **Don't Get Stuck on the Popular Options:** Most teens' choice for their first job leads to the hospitality or retail industry. However, these aren't the only choices. You could get a job in a field related to your hobbies.
- **Use Your Transferable Skills:** You might lack experience, but you have skills you can show potential employers. Many are willing to hire first-time job seekers based on their potential and talents.
- **Ask Around:** While many companies advertise their job, some don't. Tell your friends and family you're looking for a job and ask if they know an open position somewhere. Do you have friends of a similar age who recently got a job? Ask how they found it.

Prepare a CV (resume): Type and print a simple one-page document with your contact information, age, and skills. If you have a specific field or position in mind, list your skills.

- **Be Diligent:** Look for jobs through online postings, local community boards, papers, and social media. Call or visit the employers you want to work for and leave your CV.
- **Clean Up Your Social Media:** Many employers or managers look up potential employees online before hiring them. So, delete anything you wouldn't want them to see or could make you look unprofessional.

- **Ask for References**: Even without a previous employment history, you can always ask people (teachers, family friends, coaches, etc.) to vouch for your skills.

Work Readiness Skills

Improving the following work readiness skills is another way to ensure you can find a job:

- **Timekeeping**: Work on completing your tasks on time and maintain a steady schedule even if you don't have school. It helps establish a routine that transfers good timekeeping skills to the workplace.
- **Improve Your Vocabulary**: It sets a higher standard for your writing and speaking skills and opens many more doors. Reading a lot, not using words you don't understand, and expanding your oral skills make impressing potential employers easier.
- **Volunteer**: Engaging in community and volunteer services adds to your list of experiences. Volunteering is one of the best ways to showcase your skills when you don't have an employment history or experience.

Map Navigation and Direction Principles Basics

It's important to know how to read a map.
https://unsplash.com/photos/world-map-poster-9-xfYKAI6ZI?utm_content=creditShareLink&utm_medium=referral&utm_source=unsplash

The fundamental elements of a map are:

- **Title**: Look at this first to see if you have the right map for the location.
- **Scale**: Portrays the distance ratio between the map and the ground. It helps determine how far you must go.

- **Legend:** Shows the symbols on the map and what they represent.
- **Compass:** Shows the orientation of the direction East, West, North and South.
- **Latitude and Longitude:** A line system depicting a location between East and West (latitude) and North and South (longitude).

Start exploring different maps based on your interests with this information. For example, if you like hiking, find a specific location on the map, then use a map to get there (make sure an adult accompanies you). Or, use maps to explore public transportation lines to be more proficient in navigating city life.

Section 10: The Online World

In this final section, you'll learn everything about social media and the internet to become a responsible and informed social media consumer. You'll read about digital literacy and its importance and receive tips for protecting online privacy and combating cyberbullying. You'll learn to balance screen time with other, more productive activities. Lastly, you'll be advised on handling peer pressure on social media.

Digital Literacy, What It Means and Why Is It Crucial?

The digital world offers plenty of opportunities for learning and socializing. However, it can be perilous without understanding how technology works. Digital literacy helps you overcome the pitfalls of digital technology and consume online content safely and responsibly. There's much more to this world than messaging friends on social media and uploading selfies.

Digital literacy means finding, creating, and using information on the internet that doesn't harm you or anyone else. It signifies you understand where the limits and dangers lie so you can be cautious when navigating the online world.

In a world laced with digital technology, these skills are essential not only for your social life and fun but also for school and work. Digital skills are required in many schools and workplaces.

Digital literacy includes knowing how to navigate social media.
https://www.pexels.com/photo/person-holding-iphone-showing-social-networks-folder-607812/

The basic steps of digital literacy include knowing how to navigate social media and other websites and checking and sending emails. You'll be expected to create a document, research the internet, and send an assignment or answer to an inquiry via email at some point in school and work.

Next, you must learn about internet safety, cyberbullying, plagiarism, and digital footprints. If you use social media, you must know how it works, its dangers, and how to avoid them. For example, you must ensure you won't leave behind digital footprints exposing you to dangerous people or situations. A step further is creating your content, whether a blog, an app, or code.

The fundamental principles of digital literacy are:

- **Assembly:** It allows you to find, save, and organize online information or access it more easily (like saving pins on Pinterest).

- **Comprehension:** While researching information, you must understand what you're reading to evaluate whether it will be useful and identify misinformation. Doing thorough research and looking up the same information in various sources is a great way to practice this skill.

- **Social Skills:** Social factors also affect how you use digital media safely and responsibly. For example, when sending messages, you must always consider whether they're appropriate for your topic and how the person on the receiving end will perceive them. Inappropriate messages or interpretations can cause a lot of misunderstandings and hurt feelings.

- **Being Connected:** Nowadays, every part of digital media is connected in some way or shape. Not only can you access the same media through different platforms, but everything you enter online will make its way to the different channels.

How to Protect Your Online Privacy

After mastering digital literacy basics, learning to protect your online privacy is a good idea. It means filtering the information you share and whom you share it with. Below are some of the best ways to shield yourself while navigating the online world.

Use Strong Passwords

A strong password is the most powerful defense in the digital world. Generate passwords you can remember and use different ones across the various sites and apps. However, don't use your or a family member's birthday, name, or address. These are the easiest ones to figure out. Never share your password with anyone on the internet.

Use strong passwords on every site and app on which you share your information or which has access to information on your phone or computer (the easiest way to check those that do is by going into your phone's Settings and locating the Apps tab).

Change the Privacy Settings on Your Social Media Platforms

Changing the privacy settings on social media apps restricts who can access the information you share. In most cases, no app or website should have access to phone numbers, addresses, or other personal information. Check whether this information is hidden by looking at the social media privacy settings.

Think Twice Before You Send

Before you send something (whether information about yourself, anyone else, or photos or videos), think about whether it's the right thing to do. Would you share it with a friend or family member? If not, you probably shouldn't send it. Are you sending it because you're angry or upset? Did someone ask you to share it, saying they'll be mad if you don't? Neither of the latter situations is appropriate to share sensitive or personal information. Once you do, you cannot control what happens to it. You cannot take it down, so avoiding this in the first place is best.

Look at the Profiles

Getting a new friend request is exciting. However, always check the person's profile before accepting their request. See if you have common friends, where they live, how many pictures they have, etc. Dangerous people often pretend to be teens, and it's difficult to determine if someone tells the truth. Don't accept friend requests from people you don't have common friends with, who live far away, or only have a profile picture and nothing else posted on their profile.

Be Careful with Invitations and Offers

If you receive an invitation to a group on social media, check whether you have friends in that group. If not, ask if someone knows anything about the group and their opinion. Be careful when accepting invitations from groups or events. Don't go to live events you've been invited to alone. Likewise, be cautious about online jobs, internships, or study offers. They're likely a scam if you haven't previously applied for them or inquired about them. Even if you applied, don't go to an interview alone. Ask an adult to go with you instead.

Learn Cybersecurity Basics

Cybersecurity entails using specific tools to protect your online privacy. Learn to use a VPN (Virtual Private Network) to shield your location and password managing programs to keep your information safe with unhackable passwords.

Cyberbullying and How to Combat It

Cyberbullying means bullying someone through online channels, like audio and video platforms, digital messaging apps, email, or social media. For example, if someone regularly posts comments or pictures to shame or embarrass you, they're cyberbullying you.

Other cyberbullying types include:

- **Stealing and Sharing Information without Consent:** Cyberbullies often post (sometimes humiliating or sexual) images and videos of their victims, sharing them with others. They take degrading photos or videos of the victims without their consent and share these on social media and other websites.
- **Directly Harassing the Victims:** The bullies send rude, insulting, and hurtful messages, comments, or emails to the victims. They might also incite others to engage in cyberbullying through chat groups or post offensive content on the victim's social media channels.
- **Forging and Impersonating the Victim's Information:** The bullies create fake versions of the victim's accounts and post offensive content. Or, they'll hack into the victim's account and steal or change their information. Catfishing, where a victim is lured into a relationship with a person using a fake account, is also cyberbullying.

Cyberbullying often has a long-term negative impact on a victim's life. It affects your social life and school performance, making it harder to navigate life as an adult. People who have been cyberbullied as children or teens often deal with anxiety and depression as adults. Cyberbullying makes trusting people and making long-lasting relationships harder.

How to Combat Cyberbullying?

Below are steps you can take to stop cyberbullying.

Speak Up

Unfortunately, not all teens think that being cyberbullied is a serious problem or are too embarrassed to admit falling victim to it. Others believe that adults won't view this as an issue. Many teens don't speak about being cyberbullied, not even to their parents or guardians. However, if someone harasses you online, your parents should be the first ones to know about it. They can help you stop the abuse. The bully might threaten you not to tell anyone or make things worse if they find out you did. They do this to gain more power over you. You're removing the bully's power by telling your parents, teachers, and other adults.

Don't Engage

One of the easiest ways to combat cyberbullying is to avoid engaging with the attacker. It doesn't mean you must ignore it completely, which is nearly impossible, especially in today's digital world. Instead of responding to hateful comments or posts, report it to adults. Remember, your bully's goal is to make you react. By refusing to acknowledge their claims, you're depleting their power. Block them on social media and other accounts. On most social channels, by blocking them, they can't contact or tag you or see what your mutual friends post about you.

Be Diligent about Online Posting

Cyberbullies often create fake pages using the victim's information and impersonating them while continuing their abusive behavior. Be vigilant about what you post online and who can access your posts to avoid your information getting into the wrong hands. Even if someone is already cyberbullying you, don't give them even more power over you. A strong password and setting your social media profiles to private help prevent cyberbullies from hacking your profile and posting offensive and hurtful information.

Record Everything

Save every communication with the cyberbully and their posts about you, and take screenshots or photos whenever necessary. If cyberbullying continues, the information you saved will help you prove it. Show it to your parents and other adults, including school officials (if the bully is from your school).

Don't Turn Around

Some victims of cyberbullying think the only way out is to join the bullies or become a bigger bully. However, by retaliating, you only escalate the situation. Avoid this and continue respecting other people's privacy and feelings, even if they disrespect yours.

Balancing Screen Time and Other Activities

Screen time can be a valuable part of your life when balanced with other activities contributing to your health and well-being. Here are a few tips on setting healthy limits when using your gadgets.

Set Rules for Yourself

Make it a rule to use your gadgets only in certain areas of your home and at specific times. For example, don't use it in the dining room during mealtimes, in your bedroom when studying (except for school research), or at night. Or, watch TV or check social media only when your chores and homework are done.

Another rule is only using one device at a time. If you're scrolling through your phone while watching TV, choose which activity you want to continue with. Doing both confuses your brain, and you won't focus on either.

Opt for Short Screen Time Sessions

Don't spend endless hours lounging with your gadgets. Take breaks and opt for short screen time sessions. Give your brain and eyes a chance to rest from all the digital content they're exposed to.

Set a timer if you have trouble keeping track of how much time you spend online in one sitting. You'll be reminded to take a break and move around when the timer alerts you that you've reached the end of a session. Alternatively, use natural breaks, like when you're waiting for a message, reach a level in a game, or the end of the article you've been reading to create shorter sessions.

Prioritize Physical Activity

After an hour of screen time, get up and move. Engage in physical activity for several minutes. Take a walk or play with a pet. Or, better yet, play sports with your friends. An hour of physical activity will keep your body and mind healthy.

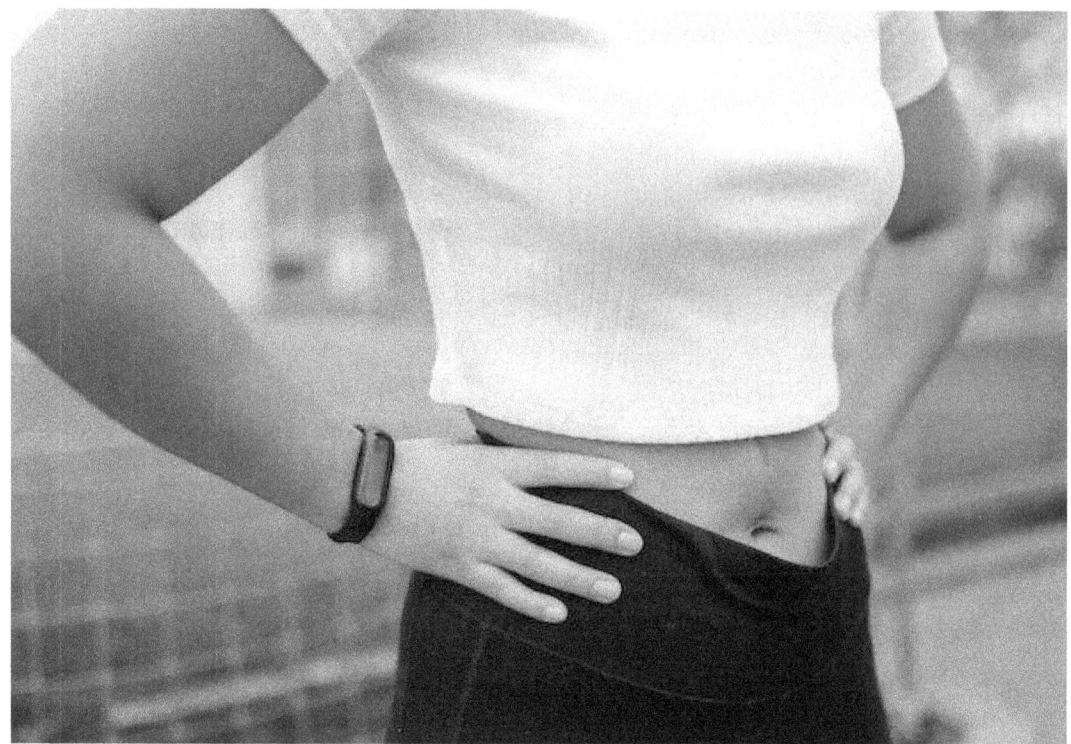

A fitness tracker will let you know how much you move through the day.
https://www.pexels.com/photo/woman-in-white-shirt-wearing-a-fitness-tracker-7746517/

A wearable activity tracker can be a great way to know how much you move through the day. It will motivate you to be more active instead of constantly submerged in the online world.

Look into Additional Extracurricular Activities

If you only know how to spend your spare time using social media, it's time to find some new extracurricular activities. This activity can be anything you enjoy doing outside of home chores and school. Whether you take up a new hobby or join a club or sports team is up to you. New activities enable you to develop new skills and make new friends. You'll have more things to do and have a better chance of balancing screen time.

Socialize and Make Friendships

Social media is a great way to create and maintain friendships, but it shouldn't be the only way. Occasionally, gather with your friends and socialize in person. Seeing them face-to-face helps you get to know them better, learn to read social cues, and build long-lasting friendships. Start by inviting your friends over or organizing a trip to the movies with friends. Don't always use your phone when spending time with your friends.

Negative Peer Pressure on Social Media

Negative peer pressure in schools and social circles is harmful enough for teenage girls. Social media creates even more damaging peer pressure, affecting your online behavior and its consequences.

Peer pressure affects you more powerfully because of the fear of missing out (FOMO). After all, if you see your friends participating in activities and challenges on social media, you don't want to miss out on them. As a result, you might engage in behavior you don't agree with or do something you're not entirely comfortable doing. You want to be cool like everyone else, so you succumb to peer pressure.

Another reason peer pressure can take hold of you is that you only see people's behavior on social media and not in real life. You compare your life with theirs, often noticing how dull yours seems compared to their exciting one. This comparison damages your self-esteem. You might emulate what these "successful" people do, even if it means engaging in risky behaviors to make your life more exciting.

Peer pressure can come in many forms. However, the most damaging consequences come from so-called "challenges" and sexting. Children and teens engage in unhealthy behaviors when doing a challenge, potentially putting their lives at risk. If you're invited to a challenge (or think about doing one), consider whether you would do it under other circumstances. Would you swallow dangerous chemicals or harm yourself in any way merely to impress someone in real life? You probably wouldn't. So, you shouldn't do it to impress anyone online, either.

Sexting refers to sharing sexual and inappropriate messages, photos, and videos with others. Many teens do it because their peers pressure them or they fear losing a person's attention. However, sexting leads to other risky behaviors, including sexual activities and excessive alcohol and drug consumption. Sexting also has other repercussions. The content you've shared can get into the hands of cyberbullies and other dangerous people. Consider these consequences before sharing sexual content with anyone.

Other Ways to Resist Peer Pressure

Here are a few suggestions for navigating peer pressure:

- **Be More Assertive:** Don't be afraid to say no or express your opinion about something you disagree with. But do it respectively.
- **Work on Your Self-Esteem:** Make a list of your strengths and abilities. Engage in activities where you use these skills. Seeing everything you're good at will make you less likely to compare yourself to others.
- **Set Personal Boundaries:** Learn your limits and let others know them. It will help you stick to your values and avoid uncomfortable situations.
- **Focus on a Supportive Social Circle:** Surround yourself with people who support your ideas and accept you for who you are.
- **Think Independently:** Learn to analyze the social trends critically. Don't embrace them without questioning them just because you see your friends or social media influencers doing them.

Thank You Message

Congratulations, you made it!

Thank you for taking the time to read this book and practice the tips and techniques mentioned. It takes courage to change your life, and you have taken the first step.

Being a teenager isn't always easy. Sometimes, you feel torn apart between wanting to fit in and the need to live the life you want. You forget about your happiness and comfort and focus on doing what society expects of you.

Every person has a unique journey and a path they should take. People are different, and no two journeys are the same. You should be proud and grateful for yours. Don't try to copy or compare yourself to others. Celebrate your one-of-a-kind personality and believe you make a difference in the world. Never change, and be proud of the person you are becoming.

Looking at your life, you will realize you have accomplished so much. Reading this book is the biggest sign you want to improve your life. However, your journey is only beginning, and so much remains to be accomplished. When you apply the skills and tips in this book, you will continue to shape your path.

You are constantly learning new things, and your journey will get more exciting. Always return to this book whenever you struggle with a problem or searching for an answer.

Good luck with what's coming. It's going to be great.

Check out another book in the series

References

(c) Copyright skillsyouneed.com 2011-. (n.d.). Personal development. Skillsyouneed.com. https://www.skillsyouneed.com/ps/personal-development.html

(c) Copyright skillsyouneed.com 2011-. (n.d.-a). Assertiveness - an introduction. Skillsyouneed.com. https://www.skillsyouneed.com/ps/assertiveness.html

(c) Copyright skillsyouneed.com 2011-. (n.d.-b). What are Social Skills? Skillsyouneed.com. https://www.skillsyouneed.com/ips/social-skills.html

(N.d.). Org.uk. https://www.mind.org.uk/information-support/types-of-mental-health-problems/self-esteem/about-self-esteem/

(N.d.-a). Apa.org. https://www.apa.org/topics/stress/anxiety-difference#:~:text=People%20under%20stress%20experience%20mental,the%20absence%20of%20a%20stressor.

(N.d.-a). Indeed.com. https://www.indeed.com/career-advice/career-development/social-skills#:~:text=Social%20skills%20are%20important%20because,position%2C%20industry%20or%20experience%20level.

(N.d.-a). Udemy.com. https://www.udemy.com/course/personal-growth-for-teens-curriculum-package-for-teachers/

(N.d.-b). Apa.org. https://www.apa.org/topics/resilience/bounce-teens

(N.d.-b). Indeed.com. https://in.indeed.com/career-advice/career-development/social-skills

(N.d.-b). Yogabasics.com. https://www.yogabasics.com/connect/yoga-blog/mind-body-connection/

(N.d.-c). Bhpioneer.com. https://www.bhpioneer.com/lifestyles/entertainment/5-actors-who-almost-quit-hollywood-before-their-big-break/video_27c26a32-e3fc-58d2-a5c7-ebce47d5824d.html

(N.d.-c). Goodtherapy.org. https://www.goodtherapy.org/blog/psychpedia/i-message

(N.d.-d). Greatexpectations.org. https://www.greatexpectations.org/wp-content/uploads/pdf/practice12/TheBenefitsofIStatements.pdf

(N.d.-e). Choosingtherapy.com. https://www.choosingtherapy.com/ambivert/#:~:text=An%20ambivert%20refers%20to%20someone,and%20when%20they're%20alone.

(N.d.-f). Apa.org. https://www.apa.org/topics/shyness#:~:text=Shyness%20is%20the%20tendency%20to,encounters%2C%20especially%20with%20unfamiliar%20people.

'Frenemies' and toxic friendships: pre-teens and teenagers. (2021, September 13). Raising Children Network. https://raisingchildren.net.au/pre-teens/behaviour/peers-friends-trends/frenemies

10 Safety Tips to Keep Your Children and Teens Safe from Harm. (n.d.). Caliber3range.Com. https://www.caliber3range.com/teen-and-child-safety

10 simple ways to cope with stress. (n.d.). Sutterhealth.org. https://www.sutterhealth.org/health/mind-body/10-simple-ways-to-cope-with-stress

10 tips teens can stay safe online. (n.d.). Unicef.Org. https://www.unicef.org/armenia/en/stories/10-tips-teens-can-stay-safe-online

10 ways to practice positive self-talk. (2021, April 23). Del. Psych. Services. https://www.delawarepsychologicalservices.com/post/10-ways-to-practice-positive-self-talk

10 ways to practice self-acceptance. (n.d.). Kids Help Phone. https://kidshelpphone.ca/get-info/10-ways-practice-self-acceptance/

5 facts about goal setting. (n.d.). Kidshealth.org. https://kidshealth.org/en/teens/goals-tips.html

5 First Aid Skills You Can Teach Your Child at Home. (2021, January 22). First Aid Course Sydney. https://thefirstaidcoursesydney.com.au/blog/5-first-aid-skills-you-can-teach-your-child-at-home/

5 Ideas for Better Sleep. (n.d.). Kidshealth.Org. https://kidshealth.org/en/teens/tips-sleep.html

5 Tips for Teaching Young Kids to Comparison Shop – bankaroo: virtual bank for kids. (n.d.). Bankaroo.Com. https://www.bankaroo.com/5-tips-for-teaching-young-kids-to-comparison-shop/

5 ways to know your feelings better. (n.d.). Kidshealth.org. https://kidshealth.org/en/teens/emotional-awareness.html

5 ways to teach your teens healthy boundaries. (2023, May 11). Youth Villages. https://youthvillages.org/5-ways-to-teach-your-teens-healthy-boundaries/

7 ways to help your teen strengthen their friendships. (n.d.). Reachout.com. https://parents.au.reachout.com/common-concerns/everyday-issues/things-to-try-peer-pressure/help-your-teenager-make-great-friends

8 ways to help your teen stop procrastinating. (n.d.). Psychology Today. https://www.psychologytoday.com/intl/blog/promoting-empathy-your-teen/202210/8-ways-help-your-teen-stop-procrastinating

All About Periods. (n.d.). Kidshealth.Org. https://kidshealth.org/en/teens/menstruation.html

Ambassador, Y. (2022, September 1). 5 ways to improve your work readiness. Youth Employment UK. https://www.youthemployment.org.uk/5-ways-to-improve-your-work-readiness/

Arlin Cuncic, M. A. (2010, May 10). 7 active listening techniques to practice in your daily conversations. Verywell Mind. https://www.verywellmind.com/what-is-active-listening-3024343

Assertiveness. (n.d.). Kidshealth.org. https://kidshealth.org/en/teens/assertive.html

Barnett, H. (2018, July 13). 24 Essential Cooking & Baking Skills Your Teen Should Know. SheKnows. https://www.sheknows.com/food-and-recipes/articles/1140231/cooking-skills-for-teens/

Barrell, A. (2020, April 24). Stress vs. anxiety: Differences, symptoms, and relief. Medicalnewstoday.com. https://www.medicalnewstoday.com/articles/stress-vs-anxiety

Battles, M. (2016, December 19). 15 ways to practice positive self-talk for success. Lifehack. https://www.lifehack.org/504756/self-talk-determines-your-success-15-tips

Being assertive: Reduce stress, communicate better. (2022, May 13). Mayo Clinic. https://www.mayoclinic.org/healthy-lifestyle/stress-management/in-depth/assertive/art-20044644

Bernhagen, K. T. (2012, February 2). Just say thanks: Why accepting compliments is good for your career. The Muse. https://www.themuse.com/advice/just-say-thanks-why-accepting-compliments-is-good-for-your-career

Betz, M. (n.d.). What is self-awareness, and why is it important? Betterup.com. https://www.betterup.com/blog/what-is-self-awareness

Breit, C. (2018, August 27). The surprising benefits of being an introvert. Time. https://time.com/5373403/surprising-benefits-introvert/

Brickel, R. E. (2020, March 28). The importance of accepting compliments. PsychAlive. https://www.psychalive.org/the-importance-of-accepting-compliments/

British Heart Foundation. (2023, December 6). Active listening. British Heart Foundation. https://www.bhf.org.uk/informationsupport/heart-matters-magazine/wellbeing/how-to-talk-about-health-problems/active-listening

Bromberg, M. (n.d.). Investing for Teens: What They Should Know. Investopedia. https://www.investopedia.com/investing-for-teens-7111843

Can a Teenager Have a Bank Account? (n.d.). Chase.Com. https://www.chase.com/personal/banking/education/basics/can-a-teenager-open-a-bank-account

Carter, C. (2021, November 17). Dear teen, this is what I want you to know about friendship. Parentingteensandtweens.com. https://parentingteensandtweens.com/dear-teen-this-is-what-i-want-you-to-know-about-friendship/

Cassata, C. (2016, May 17). How to accept yourself in 8 steps. Psych Central. https://psychcentral.com/lib/ways-to-accept-yourself

CogniFit. (2017, August 17). Peer pressure: Why we feel it, how to overcome it, and can it be positive? CogniFit Blog: Brain Health News; CogniFit. https://blog.cognifit.com/peer-pressure/

Cooks-Campbell, A. (n.d.). Social skills examples: How socializing can take you to the top. Betterup.com. https://www.betterup.com/blog/social-skills-examples

Copeland, M. E. (2016, May 17). Developing a Wellness Toolbox. Psych Central. https://psychcentral.com/lib/developing-a-wellness-toolbox

Creative Team. (2021, August 18). Teaching Map Reading Skills to Kids: Toddlers through Teens. RUN WILD MY CHILD. https://runwildmychild.com/map-reading-skills/

Critical Thinking and Decision-Making: What is Critical Thinking? (n.d.). Gcfglobal.org. https://edu.gcfglobal.org/en/problem-solving-and-decision-making/what-is-critical-thinking/1/

Cross, C. (2023, September 12). Teach Your Teen How to Use Their First Checking Account. VSECU. https://www.vsecu.com/blog/teach-your-teen-how-to-use-their-first-checking-account/

Developing a wellness toolbox for your mental health. (n.d.). Hpu.edu. https://online.hpu.edu/blog/wellness-toolbox

Discovery Building Sets. (2020, June 20). What are social skills? & why are social skills important? Discovery Building Sets Blog. https://discoverybuildingsets.com/what-are-social-skills/

Emergency Funds Explained for Teens. (2022, July 4). Mydoh. https://www.mydoh.ca/learn/money-101/building-credit/emergency-funds-explained-for-teens/

Emotional intelligence. (n.d.). Psychology Today. https://www.psychologytoday.com/us/basics/emotional-intelligence

Eng, J. (2022, January 21). How to talk to kids about toxic friendships. ParentsTogether. https://parents-together.org/how-to-talk-to-kids-about-toxic-friendships/

Erin Johnston, L. (2007, April 6). How using "I feel" statements can help you communicate. Verywell Mind. https://www.verywellmind.com/what-are-feeling-statements-425163

Evolution of communication from ancient to modern times. (n.d.). Time. https://www.kalamtime.com/blog/evolution-of-communication/

Expressing thoughts and feelings effectively. (n.d.). Exforsys.com. https://www.exforsys.com/career-center/people-skills/expressing-thoughts-feelings-effectively.html

Freund, M. (2022, August 26). 33 essential coping skills for anxiety in 2023. Ness. https://nesswell.com/coping-skills-for-anxiety/

Friends and friendships: pre-teens and teenagers. (2021, September 13). Raising Children Network. https://raisingchildren.net.au/pre-teens/behaviour/peers-friends-trends/teen-friendships

Galperin, S. (2020, March 6). Social anxiety in teens: How to overcome your social anxiety. CBT Psychology. https://cbtpsychology.com/socialanxiety/

Gillette, H. (2022, April 4). Can you become more empathetic? Absolutely, and here's how. Psych Central. https://psychcentral.com/health/how-to-be-more-empathetic

Gordon, S. (2021, April 11). Everything your teen needs to know about setting boundaries. Verywell Family. https://www.verywellfamily.com/boundaries-what-every-teen-needs-to-know-5119428

Gotter, A. (2018, April 20). 4-7-8 breathing: How it works, how to do it, and more. Healthline. https://www.healthline.com/health/4-7-8-breathing

Hartney, E., & MSc, M. A. (2009, August 29). What is peer pressure? Verywell Mind. https://www.verywellmind.com/what-is-peer-pressure-22246

Hartstein, J. (2016, March 7). 5 reasons to leave your comfort zone. Hartstein Psychological Services. https://www.hartsteinpsychological.com/5-reasons-to-leave-your-comfort-zone-suhadee-sue-henriquez-lcsw-act

Hauck, C. (2018, October 11). A 10-minute meditation to work with difficult emotions. Mindful; Mindful.org. https://www.mindful.org/a-10-minute-meditation-to-work-with-difficult-emotions/

HDFS 211: Common emotions of adolescence. (n.d.). Res.In. http://ecoursesonline.iasri.res.in/mod/page/view.php?id=24402

Healthdirect Australia. (2022). Self-talk. https://www.healthdirect.gov.au/self-talk

Here are the reasons why girls need a safe space. (n.d.). Unicef.Org. https://www.unicef.org/turkiye/en/stories/here-are-reasons-why-girls-need-safe-space

Holbrook, S. (2019, July 24). Safety Tips for Teenagers Home Alone for the Evening. Your Teen Magazine. https://yourteenmag.com/family-life/communication/safety-tips-for-teens

Holmes, L. (2003, September 10). Differences between sadness and clinical depression. Verywell Mind. https://www.verywellmind.com/sadness-is-not-depression-2330492

How to Cope With Social Media Peer Pressure. (n.d.). Kidcentraltn.Com. https://www.kidcentraltn.com/health/mental-emotional-health/how-to-cope-with-social-media-peer-pressure.html

How to handle peer pressure. (n.d.-a). Fairfax County Public Schools. https://www.fcps.edu/student-wellness-tips/peer-pressure

How to handle peer pressure. (n.d.-b). Kidshealth.org. https://kidshealth.org/en/kids/peer-pressure.html

How to help teenagers make good decisions. (2020, September 2). Spark Their Future. https://www.sparktheirfuture.qld.edu.au/how-to-help-your-teen-make-good-decisions-about-school-and-life/

How to help your teen manage toxic friendships. (2023, June 23). River Oaks Psychology. https://riveroakspsychology.com/how-to-help-your-teen-manage-toxic-friendships/

How to live a happy life. (n.d.). Kidshealth.org. https://kidshealth.org/en/teens/happy-life.html

How to Read a "Drug Facts" Label. (n.d.). Nationwidechildrens.Org. https://www.nationwidechildrens.org/family-resources-education/health-wellness-and-safety-resources/helping-hands/how-to-read-a-drug-facts-label

Improving emotional intelligence (EQ) - Helpguide.org. (n.d.). https://www.helpguide.org/articles/mental-health/emotional-intelligence-eq.htm

Jane. (2019, May 27). Learning to Label My Emotions. Jane Taylor | Transition and Wellbeing Coaching | Life Coaching | Gold Coast. https://www.habitsforwellbeing.com/learning-to-label-my-emotions/

Janice Zerbe, Michigan State University Extension. (n.d.). Five tips that help teens be successful with money. 4-H. https://www.canr.msu.edu/news/five_tips_that_help_teens_be_successful_with_money

Janice Zerbe, Michigan State University Extension. (n.d.). MSU Extension. MSU Extension. https://www.canr.msu.edu/news/beginning_financial_planning_terminology

Jennifer. (2019, November 12). Consequences of choices: How do you find the best ones for your life? Contentment Questing. https://contentmentquesting.com/consequences-of-choices/

Kapadia, H. (2022, February 9). How To Establish The Right Hair Care Routine For Teenagers. MyCocoSoul. https://mycocosoul.com/blogs/hair-care-regimen/teenage-hair-care-routine

Kaspersky. (2023, September 8). Cyberbullying: What is it? Www.Kaspersky.Com. https://www.kaspersky.com/resource-center/preemptive-safety/top-10-ways-to-stop-cyberbullying

Kendra Cherry, M. (2013, August 2). Emotions and types of emotional responses. Verywell Mind. https://www.verywellmind.com/what-are-emotions-2795178

Kendra Cherry, M. (2014, April 17). 5 signs you might be an extrovert. Verywell Mind. https://www.verywellmind.com/signs-you-are-an-extrovert-2795426

Kendra Cherry, M. (2015, January 5). Why empathy is important. Verywell Mind. https://www.verywellmind.com/what-is-empathy-2795562

Khona, M. (2020, October 19). 16 Effective Skin Care Tips For Teenagers. SkinKraft. https://skinkraft.com/blogs/articles/skin-care-tips-for-teenagers

Kid's Health Team. (2017, June 30). Independent teens: 9 safety tips for going out alone. Shine365. https://shine365.marshfieldclinic.org/kids-health/independent-teens-safety-tips/

Klynn, B. (n.d.). Emotional regulation: Skills, exercises, and strategies. Betterup.com. https://www.betterup.com/blog/emotional-regulation-skills

Kubala, J., MS, & RD. (2022, June 20). Healthy Eating for Teens: What You Need to Know. Healthline. https://www.healthline.com/nutrition/healthy-eating-for-teens

Lebow, H. I. (2020, June 19). Emotion management strategies: 6 methods to try. Psych Central. https://psychcentral.com/health/ways-to-manage-your-emotions

www.ingramcontent.com/pod-product-compliance
Lightning Source LLC
Chambersburg PA
CBHW081353040426
42450CB00016B/3423